SAIPAN

JOHN CIARDI
as Aviation Cadet

S A I P A N

THE WAR DIARY
OF JOHN CIARDI

Introduction by Edward M. Cifelli

Foreword by Robert M. "Mac" Cordray

The University of Arkansas Press

Fayetteville   London   1988

Designer: Chiquita Babb
Typeface: Linotron 202 Ehrhardt
Typesetter: G & S Typesetters, Inc.
Printer: McNaughton & Gunn, Inc.
Binder: John H. Dekker & Sons, Inc.

The paper used in this publication meets the minimum
requirements of the American National Standard for
Permanence of Paper for Printed Library Materials
Z39.48-1984. ∞

Library of Congress Cataloging-in-Publication Data
Ciardi, John, 1916–1986
  Saipan :   the war diary of John Ciardi.
  1. Ciardi, John, 1916–1986—Diaries. 2. Poets,
American—20th century—Diaries. 3. World War,
1939–1945—Personal narratives, American. I. Title.
PS3505.I27Z475 1988   818'.5403 [B]   87-25564
ISBN 1-55728-017-7 (alk. paper)
ISBN 1-55728-018-5 (pbk.)

Table of Contents

List of Illustrations

Introduction

John Ciardi on Saipan

"I thought war was raucous and close mouthed and rigidly exact and that all men close to the fighting and dying were obscene as Marine Sgts. and hard as Hollywood desperadoes. I believed that in my fearful innocence. I never dreamed that there was gentleness and tenderness and confessed fear everywhere in it. I could never have dreamed the tenderness that breeds in war."

13 February 1945

Saipan is the wartime journal of John Ciardi. It is a warm and personal document, filled with a soldier's everyday concerns at one moment and with an artist's enduring ones the next. We read, for example, that the collective weight of Ciardi's twelve-man B-29 crew was 2,910 pounds; but we also read of a discussion with a soldier named Levin which leads Ciardi to a forthright statement of his sticking point with religion: "There's something I just can't swallow about immortality." This counterpoint between commonplace observation and intellectual musing marks the diary as it also marks Ciardi's later life and his greatest poetry. In an Emersonian sense, John Ciardi took large meanings from everyday sources, going so far in this direction as to name one of his books *The Little That Is All* (1974).

Saipan, however, is first a war diary. It presents vivid images of men at war and is characterized by numerous physical descriptions (of men, places, and battles) as well as equally frequent psychological penetrations. Moments of great dramatic intensity are recorded, too, as we read of the life-and-death tension experienced by all soldiers at war, by the particular members of his crew, and certainly by himself as well. Finally, by the way the diary more or less drifts at the end into uncertain silences, we not only come to understand but experience the sense of impending doom John Ciardi felt. This is a book of great personal discovery, a revealing study of a man learning under fire about some part of himself that he had not known existed.

The diary covers the period between early November 1944 and mid-March 1945. At the beginning, Ciardi had been self-assured and confident. On 27 November, in the midst of a Japanese aerial attack, he had watched a crew chief drive a tractor onto a runway and tow his plane to safety. The sight had been so movielike as to reinforce a simply felt idea of bravery: "I like to think of our men doing things like that. It's good to have courage—nothing happens to the brave." But by February, a restrained anger had set in: "We were on the Island [Saipan] to destroy Japanese factories and Japanese factories had a price tag attached. We were the price and neither longing nor the will to live mattered in the final balance." By mid-March the sense of death had become heavy, and it is clear that Ciardi saw little hope for survival. He later wrote very forthrightly, "I did not expect to get off Saipan alive."*

Ciardi's last diary entry was 10 March. It was as though the daily or even weekly recording of his last days grew to be too much for him. There was an unmistakable doom waiting for him somewhere in the Pacific, and reading these last entries

*Jeffry Lovill, "The Poetry of John Ciardi: How Does it Mean?" Diss., Arizona State University, 1985. 337. Other quotations from John Ciardi not found in the diary may be located in "About Being Born, and Surviving It," ed. Adele Sarkissian, *Contemporary Authors Autobiography Series* (Detroit, Michigan: Gale Research Company 1985) 2: 79–96.

today, we are left with the same desperation and heaviness of spirit John Ciardi felt at that moment.

However, some time after the last entry (the exact date was not recorded), John Ciardi was reassigned to a desk job—his life unexpectedly spared. He would spend six more months on Saipan, but combat missions were over. Had Ciardi been a religious man, he might well have thought a miracle had saved him. As it was, he attributed survival to simple good luck, the kind no one in his position had a right to expect. He put it this way: "In the end it was luck—and poetry—that saved me."

Luck and Poetry

The story of John Ciardi on Saipan, and how poetry saved him, perhaps begins with his graduation from Tufts in 1938, long before he realized that he and his generation would be drawn into world war. He had had the wonderful good fortune at Tufts to discover the quintessential poetry teacher, John Holmes, a man whom Ciardi regarded for the rest of his life as a surrogate father and an artistic torchbearer. It was Holmes who suggested to the young graduate that he pack his belongings and head for the University of Michigan. There he was to enroll in a graduate program in creative writing, study under Roy W. Cowden, and compete for the Hopwood Award in poetry. Holmes had even arranged (through some professor friends at Michigan) a scholarship and part-time job for his young protégé. In the summer of 1938, then, John Ciardi looked westward from Massachusetts with a magna cum laude degree in his pocket, an unbridled enthusiasm for poetry, and lofty goals in his sights.

At Michigan Ciardi found even greater success; certainly it was more rewarding. In June 1939, he won the Hopwood, which carried a cash award of $1,200, and he also took his master's degree. Any one of these would have provided just cause for celebration. As he said, "Lucky John was rich!"—in more ways than one.

After paying back some four hundred dollars of graduate school debts, split evenly between his Godfather John Follo and his sister Ella, Lucky John drifted to the West Coast and back again to Ann Arbor. The six months of exploration must have been fun, for he returned in January 1940 with no money, no job, and no prospects. Even then, however, other good things were brewing.

John Holmes had shown a revised copy of Ciardi's Hopwood-winning manuscript to William Sloane, then trade manager at Henry Holt. Sloane sent a one hundred dollar cash advance, and Ciardi's first book of poems did, indeed, appear in 1940, under the title *Homeward to America.* Sloane also arranged a fellowship for the young poet at Bread Loaf in August. On another front, Louis Untermeyer, who had been at Michigan in 1938–39, had gone off to teach at the University of Kansas City in September 1940. Untermeyer suggested to President Clarence R. Decker that the recent Hopwood winner from Michigan might like to join the faculty as a guest lecturer in Modern Poetry. Last minute arrangements were made, and Ciardi went off to the Middle West for $900 per semester. For the better part of the next two years, it proved to be a good life: "I was on a university faculty, I was making a living, at twenty-three I wasn't much older than the senior girls, I had time to write, and I was bursting with ignorant energy."

In 1942, however, fearful of being drafted into the infantry, John Ciardi joined the aviation cadets. Early testing at Nashville had washed him out of pilot training consideration and established navigation as his field. While he waited for a spot in navigation school to open, Ciardi returned to his home for six long months—with no pay. Finally, in late 1942, he was called. He attended the school and qualified as a navigator; he had even been given his honorable discharge as a necessary step before receiving his commission. On the day before the scheduled commissioning, however, Ciardi was called back and made a private again. Something had gone wrong.

It seems that as a graduate student at Michigan, Ciardi had lined up against the fascists in the Spanish War. He had had his head turned slightly to the left by his classmates, many of whom had fought the fascists in Spain and returned to talk of it. He recalled later that he had been "a bit awed by their war experiences and persuaded by what they foresaw." The heady experience of his Michigan year, poetically and politically, moved him to sign "every zany petition the loonies" put before him. It was this indiscriminate petition-signing that was turned up by a House un-American Affairs committee. It cost John Ciardi his commission as an officer.

But it also saved his life. Every man with whom Ciardi had trained at navigation school was shortly afterward reported either killed or missing in action. Thus, John Ciardi alone survived, and that only because, in Army logic, all anti-fascists must by definition be pro-communists—and therefore not officer material. The fact that Army logic should have saved his life was a sweet irony for Ciardi to turn over in his mind and savor through the rest of his life. "Lucky John" would never have imagined that good fortune might come from such a quarter. But it was so.

The Army had moved John Ciardi back to square one. His navigation training was put aside as his commission had been, and he found himself in May 1944 at Lowry Field in Denver, training to be a gunner. To be more precise, he was at Central Fire Control School where he learned to handle the electronically controlled guns on a B-29. By October he had become one member of a twelve-man crew that was learning to operate as a single unit, a life-support team. They had formed and trained at Walker Army Air Base at Hayes, Kansas, and finally came together with the Crew Chief at the air base in Kearney, Nebraska, where the crews learned to work together and where they prepared themselves for overseas duty.

". . . the instinct for self preservation kicks up."

John Ciardi began his war journal on 5 November 1944, as a response to a letter he had received from his friend Ted Morrison. It suddenly occurred to him that the Army might be seen as a stage upon which the "human situation" could be observed. But it was a curious business at best, he realized, because in the Army "no one acts like himself." The clarity of this perception illuminates not only the Army, but oddly the diary as well, because very slowly from November to March we see John Ciardi emerge as a man. For, in a sense, by discovering layers of himself that perhaps he had not known about, he slowly began to act like himself—like the sensitive artist caught in a deadly dilemma. By March 1945, the real John Ciardi, as he had never been seen before, is laid bare in the diary pages.

What, then, was he at the beginning of the diary if not himself? The answer, of course, is that for patriotism's sake he had temporarily forsaken, in a manner of speaking, his artistic nature to become a soldier. Certainly one of the most human, and therefore one of the best, aspects of the journal is Ciardi's growing awareness of his own mortality and his outright admission of fear. The diary traces his transformation back again from soldier to man, from mission-oriented gunner into a warmly human man who happened as well to be a poet. This reawakening of a sort will be for many readers the diary's most moving dimension. It may well be that this image of John Ciardi as a frightened and vulnerable man is a truer picture than the one of him as an articulate B-29 gunner.

Certainly, John Ciardi was as articulate as a diary writer as he was later in his various literary careers. The first part of the diary, from early November to early December, follows Ciardi and the crew from Kearney, Nebraska to Saipan. This section is forward-looking and marked by what might be described as restless energy. On Saipan in late November, the crew hears rumors about missions that may have been lost, and they experience Japanese attacks. Ciardi describes several air raids and the things the men thought about, talked about, and did. By early December, he is eager for action. "I would like," he says, "to get over a target—even Tokio. Well, maybe, tomorrow."

The wait for their first mission ended on 3 December 1944 at 4:30 in the morning. The entry for that day is long and detailed, filled with one obvious type of war excitement. They were finally doing what they had all been trained for, what they had somewhat nervously waited for. For Ciardi, of course, the wait had been especially long, and perhaps for that reason it was especially satisfying. He recorded it this way after the battle:

> I was cockeyed proud of the crew. Not a rattle in the bunch. The interphone clicked off the attacks easily and accurately. Every man was functioning calmly and well and it was a proud thing to know. This is the pilot's air corps, but it takes eleven men to fly a 29. [The twelfth is the Ground Crew Chief.] And eleven men have to lose their fear and be sure of themselves before a crew can function. We functioned.

For the moment at least, it might be said of John Ciardi, as it was of Henry Fleming in *The Red Badge of Courage,* that he "had been to touch the great death, and found that, after all, it was but the great death."

The next two weeks were passed in the afterglow of his initial success. The missions went well and the diary is filled with colorful battle scenes, vivid characterizations, and a touristy (perhaps even anthropological) description of the natives. But on 7 December, he received mail "and found in it a $100 check from *Poetry Magazine* with notice of having been awarded the Eunice Tietjens Memorial Prize for 1944. . . . The prize is given this year for the first time. I like being the one to start it." This notice, finding him as it did halfway across the world and in the midst of a war, was a dramatic reminder of the world of poetry. It was one thing, he realized, to write poems and keep notebooks under the stress of war; it was quite another to be back home taking his rightful place among the promising young poets of his time. It must have been a wonder to him that somehow poetry had tracked him down and made him remember a literary time before the war. The possibility of not returning, of dying in the Pacific, was terrible enough in its own right, but the thought of leaving unfulfilled a hoped-for literary destiny added anguish to his pain. One might reasonably argue that it was a cruel turn of fate that allowed long-anticipated mail to contain the kind of news that would threaten Ciardi's cultivated soldier's demeanor, his military thick skin.

It may have been coincidental, but little more than a week later, a crack in the armor appeared: "Somewhere in the last few days time swallowed and disappeared. It began with one of those sudden chemical anxieties. Chemical because there was no rational part of me in it. We were put up for a mission to Nagoya and suddenly I dreaded it. It made a sleepless night and left me cursing mad in the morning. . . ." He was looking directly at that sleepless night and into his own fear, and then he threw off a typical Ciardi quip with typical Ciardi honesty: "It takes a little time for me to get used to going to sleep at night knowing that I may be killed the next day. Ideally, I'd like to be unmoved by it, but I can't quite seem to manage it."

He had to manage through 22 December, but from then until 14 January, Ciardi's plane (dubbed after their first bombing mission as the *Heavenly Body*) was grounded for repairs. During that time, he began thinking about chance. It seems that a friend of his from another crew had a wound that kept him from flying on a mission from which his crew never returned. Ciardi then mused about chance: "no precaution in the world will rule out the overwhelming and forever impact of possibility and impossibility that can happen to you." He thought further of the "smiling boys" who died. And finally, with simplicity and honesty, John Ciardi seems to have discovered for himself a time-honored truth: "I don't know. I don't think I'll mind it [his own death] too much. The trouble with wakening the imagination is that it makes you afraid in advance."

Yet of all the triggers that caused John Ciardi to face his own mortality, it may have been the filmed life of George Gershwin, *Rhapsody in Blue,* that had the greatest effect. He admired the film's photography, but of course it was the music that touched him—and possibly drove the soldier prematurely out of his body:

> It was a strong thing to hear Gershwin again. It's too terrific. It fascinated me and suddenly it scared me. I don't want to see it again. I don't know what this sudden flood of hypersensitivity is, but somewhere it flipped a lid and scared me. I listened to the Rhapsody in Blue and thought that I didn't want to die, and came back to find a new man (MacMillan) sleeping in what had been Hodge's bed, and it scared me.

Clearly, it was art that had triggered his response; it was the re-realization that his future, barring a premature end in the Pacific, was to have been spent in the service of poetry. When the dual realities of art and war impinged on his consciousness in a way that he could not ignore, he became frightened, frightened that he would never again return to the world of letters.

Then, with his fears already apparent, the final straw was added. He wrote on 21 January: "Nothing changes until it gets worse." The Army decided to break up his crew. The support system that had trained as a unit and fought as a unit, the one that had made John so "cockeyed proud," was breaking up. Mac Cordray, the pilot and heart of the crew, was "going up to Wing to fly a super-Dumbo," and other moves were rumored. Ciardi didn't like it: "if it goes through as first reports have it, I can't see flying." A couple of days later, he uncharacteristically referred to himself in the third person: "Ciardi seems to be having combat nerves." In the end, his fears seemed to merge: ". . . the instinct for self preservation kicks up. I find myself thinking that it's foolish to stick my neck out over Japan when my real usefulness and capability as a person and as a unit of society is in writing what needs to be written well." By early February, the *Heavenly Body* itself was taken from them, and they were forced to share another B-29, the *Slick Dick,* with some other crew. John Ciardi's spirits were near rock bottom.

Toward the end of February, shortly before he gave up the diary, Ciardi had a hard time keeping up his inner strength. In an undated entry, he said simply, "I am not a soldier." He saw himself as "a civilian accepting the risks and restrictions necessary to doing a job that must be done before I can return to my own patterns." But the possibility of returning to his own patterns seemed to be getting more and more remote. He tried to reconcile himself to it and was driven finally to writing a letter home in case he did not make it back. And then the Army made it worse. Crews were ordered to fly low altitude missions, which meant that the B-29s would be vulnerable to attacks from above as well as below. He wondered if "Wing's refusal to tell us how many missions we're to fly means that we're here to be used up."

It was in this near-desperate state of mind that he began seeing himself and the others on Saipan simply as the price tag for the destruction of some Japanese factories. There was a commonly felt sense of impending disaster: "We cannot stop the fear."

Grammarian

John Ciardi later recorded that at just this time, when his own personal war was at its bleakest, he returned from an especially frightening mission to find that he had been ordered to Headquarters. It seems that a personnel officer needed what he called a "grammarian." He searched through the personnel files and discovered that John Ciardi was a writer; then, as luck would have it, a recent issue of *Atlantic* with some Ciardi poems came to his attention. And that settled it. John Ciardi was forthwith reassigned to Headquarters. His duties included writing up awards and citations as well as letters of condolence to the families of men killed in action. He saw his work as a sort of public relations job for General Rosie O'Donnell. In the end, though, it was, indeed, luck and poetry that had saved him.

Three missions after John Ciardi had been reassigned to desk duty, the remaining members of his original crew were lost in a direct hit over Tokyo Bay. Against all odds, Army logic had saved him again—this time because some unidentified officer figured poets must be grammarians. It had been exactly this sort of randomness, this sort of blind luck, that had contributed so largely to his fears in the first place. He had written on 16 February, after having survived a foolhardy mission over Nagoya, "So we live. (With luck. Without luck, it's so we die.)"

John Ciardi spent some six additional months on Saipan, buffered from real danger by mountains of paper. Why did he not resume the diary? The answer is likely to be found in the intensity of his entries during February and March. When he began the diary on 5 November 1944, looking for aspects of the "human situation" in the Army, he could not have foreseen that the most human situation he would discover was the fear in his own heart. The overpowering reality of that fear and the incredible good fortune that took him out of harm's way in the nick of time seemed to argue against continuing the diary. Perhaps he was simply too emotionally drained to continue. Perhaps he could not find it within himself to juxtapose life and death war entries with more or less trivial business office entries. The Saipan drama was over for him, and continuing the diary would only have diminished the self-discoveries that had surfaced. I suspect John Ciardi realized all this and realized also that the diary's abrupt ending had a special poignancy all its own.

But John Ciardi was not finished with the war quite yet. He had two responsibilities to fulfill—one military and one poetic. His military responsibilities from April through September were not terribly demanding. He undoubtedly saw it as an opportunity to get his emotional life back in order. As part of his work on awards and decorations he made frequent flights to Guam reporting to Air Force Brass there. It was rewarding work: he kept his flight pay (fifty percent over base pay) and was courted by gift-giving military types eager for awards. Less pleasant, of course, were the letters of condolence, among which—as a last ironic twist—were those he had to write to the families of the men from his own crew. He was still Lucky John, but now he did not so much exult as ponder the capriciousness of fortune.

Some men might have lived long enough to forget their good fortune. Not so John Ciardi. He approached the rest of his life as an opportunity to do the literary things he had nearly been cheated of. He worked with incredible energy to make his saved life one worthwhile, personally and poetically. And his enormous achievement in the world of modern American letters will remain a living testament to the life that was miraculously spared on Saipan.

Ciardi's first post-war contribution to American letters was, in fact, a wrapping up of his poetic responsibilities felt during the war. In 1947 he published *Other Skies*, a volume of war poems. Several of these poems, plus some later ones taken from his Saipan experience, are available today in *Selected Poems* (1984). Of particular interest is "The Graph" from Ciardi's poetic autobiography, *Lives of X* (reprinted also in *Selected Poems*). Finally, at the end of this volume are a handful of poems that were included in the diary, some of which are published here for the first time. All these poems take on a new light in connection with the diary. The overwhelming prose honesty of the diary provides a new entrance to the poems, many of which have long stood among Ciardi's best.

When John Ciardi wrote in the diary that there was something about the idea of immortality that he could not swallow, he was, of course, speaking in religious terms. It is a lovely irony that so much of what he wrote will achieve for him a kind of earthly immortality, which—although he said later in his life that he had outlived ambition—is an immortality he could surely accept.

Edward M. Cifelli
Lake Lenape, N J
5 November 1987

Foreword

I don't remember the exact day when I met John Ciardi. I know it was some time during the spring when a large number of us were assembled at a hastily built air base in the middle of Kansas between Hayes and Victoria to begin what for some of us promised to be a great adventure and to others simply an unpleasant job that was interrupting our lives. But we knew we were there to do a job our fathers thought they had finished.

I'm not certain how John and I came to be on the same crew. I liked to think I had some hand in the selection of my crew members, but chance probably had more to do with it.

Immature and too conscious that I was an officer and John an enlisted man, I nevertheless, though somewhat reluctantly, became his friend. A small group of us, both officers and enlisted men, used to gravitate to the mess hall after "lights out" to cadge food and coffee from the night cook. We talked about many things, but most of our nightly sessions eventually became classrooms with John trying, generally unsuccessfully, to share with us the why of poetry. I came to learn that a man is measured by more than the stripes on his sleeve or the bars on his shoulder.

Four of us from that original crew survived, a little wiser and a great deal more experienced in the ways of living and dying, to become life-long friends. John was always the one who kept track of the rest of us. For this I am grateful.

As I attempted to identify the people, places, terms, and things in his diary, I found that many old memories came back; some I would rather not have had brought to mind. But, whether pleasant or unpleasant, John's entries were honest and fair. He portrayed me as a perfectionist who did not suffer incompetence or stupidity calmly, and this is true, though with some slow-earned wisdom I have become more mellow in the intervening forty years.

The diary stops abruptly in the middle of March 1945, more than six months before we came home. But this did not mark the end of John's account of his experiences. Some of what happened he told in the short autobiography, "About Being Born, and Surviving It" included in *John Ciardi: Measure of the Man*, edited by Vince Clemente, and published by The University of Arkansas Press in 1987. Shortly after his last entry he was pulled off the flight crew, assigned to Wing Headquarters, and set to the boring but safe task of writing commendations and letters of condolence for the general.

While he was doing this office work the plane he had been flying, with most of the crew he had flown and faced death with, was blown out of the air. Not surprisingly, John became increasingly aware of his own mortality. "Why not come fly a mission with me?," I asked him once. "I won't volunteer," he answered. "That would make me responsible for my own possible death. But you order me and I'll go."

During our last conversation in the fall of 1985, John told me that he had done all that he felt was necessary; he would accept the years allotted him, but he was prepared to die.

On Easter Sunday of 1986 he sat down in his home in Metuchen, New Jersey, and his heart stopped. May the Lord bless and keep John and give him peace.

Robert M. Cordray
Lexington, Kentucky
1988

THE

DIARY

February 1, '45

It has become (grown to be) quite a while since I made an entry. I perceive that I'm not a diary keeper by temperament. The last entry was the Nagoya mission. The early of the reports were wrong. The crew did not ditch. Their plane blew up at 8,000 ft. The Wing lost 3 others. Those that came back were shot full of holes - it's a wonder how some of them made it back at all. All praise to No. 2 Engine for stopping us.

It gave me the jitters for a while. The boys on Gowick's old crew were boys I'd known a long while. Just a few days before I had written a letter in bad Italian for Curti's mother, a letter full of the proper filial palaver that men the son loves his mother but has never been able to communicate with her in a living relationship. I remember thinking that it was a terrific waste to let a relationship become mother-and-son instead of person-to-person. Well, it's no longer a problem in this instance I'm afraid. It was wasted in matter

2

I got a letter from Ted Morrison today and answering it started a thought. He mentioned that Wally Stegner was living around in odd sections of the country doing a series of articles for *Look* magazine on foreign populations, slums, and not slums, I suppose. A sort of human study.

Which suddenly made me wonder about the Army as a human situation. It dawns on me that the Army is the last place in the world to observe human nature. The reason is, I think, that no one acts like himself: In the barracks you live mostly by whatever forty odd men may have in common—mostly dice, cards, profanity, sleep, and smuggled whiskey. Out on the town there's too much loneliness, disassociation, and whatever the word is for the compulsion of time—the feeling that all your life must be squeezed into tonight on this street under these neons over this glass in the blare of this juke box and this girl's flesh.

So far the Army has been one of two things—long boring intervals of nothing to do, or long endless spells of too much to do. Neither leaves much chance for one to be himself.

I find myself behaving strangely for me. I think I miss the lack of privacy. There never seems to be time to stop and think.

This for example is the unexpurgated history of a 38 hour pass:

The orderly room bulletin board read "All overnight passes good for 24 hours or until next duty." Since "next duty" meant nothing except that I had to be available at 7:00 AM Monday morning, I found myself with 38 free hours. And since we're about ready to go overseas, it seemed a perfect last chance for a tub and a bed with sheets. I lathered myself into town to the Fort Kearney Hotel and the Midway. No rooms. No rooms with bath. No rooms without bath. No rooms. I thought three quick thoughts involving axes, hand grenades,

3

and slow torture and went philosophically up the street to make the dinner the Capt. was throwing for the crew.

At 6:30 we were finally assembled only an hour late—The Skipper, Orenstein, Grow, O'Hara, Campbell, Franklin, Saloz, Johnson, Blakely, me, and Smith (crew chief). Moore is going overseas via ATC and won't be with us till we meet him there.

We had a good steak, all the talk that 12 men on a crew can have in common (whiskey, women and airplanes) and O'Hara, Campbell, Saloz and I had too much to drink. Saloz amused himself by spiking my rum and coke on the sly. It wasn't until I had passed the point of caring that I discovered why my drink seemed to get stronger as it grew shorter.

In the course of dinner we compiled the following statistics.

1) Average age of crew—25 years and one month (Johnson 22, Orenstein 22, Saloz 23, O'Hara and Blakely 24, Captain 25, Grow 26, Campbell and Franklin 27, Moore, Smith, and Ciardi 28). I just make it as oldest man on the crew.

2) Domestic status: five married, six single, one (Blakely) half and half.

3) Parenthood: Moore—2 girls, Smith—I forget, Campbell—1 girl, Grow—1 boy, Saloz—waiting.

4) Moustaches—Capt. Blakely, Campbell. Had moustaches but reformed—O'Hara, Franklin, Ciardi.

5) Total weight of crew—2910 lbs.

That much vital information and 12 steaks compiled we all made pretty speeches to each other, decided all over again that we're the best crew in the business—which of course we are—and made vows for the future. The Captain ended up with three resolutions: 1) That he would fly as briefed and get back, 2) That there would be no avoidable heroics, 3) That he would guarantee us no decorations but a theatre ribbon. We all shouted, loved each other very much, and got up—mostly drunk.

4

I was drunk enough to need ballast. I sat down and ate another steak. It was a good steak and I began to settle back into focus enough to launch myself to the phone. I called DP and we went to Ben's Club and danced until 1:00 while I proceeded to get out of focus again on brandy. Not too much so, however. The outside air removed the double image effect and I took DP home and settled down for the end of a soldier's evening. I wasn't too sure that I wanted anything as strenuous as sex, but the uniform seemed to demand it.

As a matter of fact neither of us seemed to be able to make up the other's mind. According to Air Force Memorandum 2–5–716 (I believe) I undressed her at least four times, tampered irresolutely, bumped into her final inhibitions, and bowed to them. I said "Goodnight" at least four times at spaced intervals and was called back "for a while." It seemed to be a tug of war between glands and inhibitions. The glands finally won, but male physiology, uniform or no uniform, is elastic only to a certain point. My glands having been boiling and cooling off all night I'm afraid she got only what I expected—a fizzle from a frazzle.

Which left me out on the streets at about 4:15 with no buses to camp until 6:30. I had an enormous urge for food with no cafes open. I finally found one and stepped into the good warm air of pancakes and coffee just in time to be told the place was off limits.

It was a logical ending. I fought my way back into the street, roamed the town for a while, and finally fell asleep in the lobby of the Midway Hotel where a beautiful dawn began when some fool shook me and said, "It's six o'clock, soldier."

What of it?

But I went.

I made it to camp by 7:00, slept until 1:00, mooched around all afternoon, spent the evening losing my last $60 at Bacarat, and from the Northeast corner of the Combat Crew

Latrine at 02:13 AM on Nov. 6, 1944, UAAF, Kearney, Nebraska—to all, a good night.

The bottom dropped out of the weather. The field has been socked in solid for two days. The card games boil in the bar-racks, the planes roar on the ground and stay there, and you can't see the barracks across the street. If it clears we'll fly a shakedown flight this afternoon.

We finally made our shakedown flight, but praise the weather. The base unit had us cleared to fly two days ago. With nothing to do we checked the ship ourselves. The clearance form was perfect. Inspection showed not enough gas and oil, dirty strainers, a flat strut, #2 engine cutting out, the upper forward turret unlatchable. We worked on it all afternoon and finally made it off just before dark. After two hours #3 engine had to be feathered and we came in with the ambulance waiting.

If they can fix it we take off tomorrow for P of E.

Two days of being socked in by the weather, a grand tussle with the Form 1A and at long last Roosevelt has been re-elected and we fly again. For the last 3 we've been scheduled for our shakedown flight after the 100 hr. inspections. When we finally got a weather clearance we took time out to inspect the plane despite a clean check-off on the Form 1A. We'd have done better to fly the Form 1A—the ship was short on gas and oil, the strainers were fouled, the left landing strut was flat, the new upper forward turret cover was not latched and improperly adjusted so that it couldn't latch, and #2 engine cut out when it was run up.

We gave her back to the line crews and the Skipper left a few patches of burning sulfur around the various line officers. We finally took her off today for a short run—two hours, mostly an air-speed calibration run. Number 3 engine kicked up in an hour and 35 minutes and had to be feathered. We came in on three engines past the disappointed meat wagon. I ate too much lunch, and I've just finished packing for shipment to P of E tomorrow.

California here I come.

NOV. 9, 1944

Take off for P of E was cancelled. Bad weather over the Rockies. We may get off tomorrow.

We washed the plane this afternoon. A nasty job, but it fairly shines and we scrubbed a lot of drag off her. When we finished O'Hara and I went to the PX for coffee. O'Hara mentioned that he'd just written his mother to tell her he was going overseas. We've known it for months, but I hadn't told Mother till a week or so ago. Not even that I was flying.

Out of curiosity I asked ten of the men if they'd kept from telling wives and mothers till the last minute. Eight said they had. I wonder why. My guess is that too many women use worrying as a device for special consideration and consequently force their men into secrecy. I think they'd be a lot smarter to share their men's lives instead of demanding their sentimentality, but I guess I've always known that's pretty much a dream.

I hope we get off tomorrow. I'm fed up on dawdling.

The security officer hauled us out of bed at 0530 for another try at clearing the field and by 0700 we and a pea-soup fog were gathered around the plane, each waiting for the other to give in. The night was freezing (it dawned about 0740) and the wet fog had frozen to the wings heavily enough to break the air-flow. We hauled mechanics' stands and an 8-pipe hot air blower and put in an hour or two crawling, slipping and sliding over the plane melting the frost off the wings and tail plane. The slipping and sliding, incidentally, is serious business—a 16 or 18 foot fall off a wing onto a concrete runway is not the healthiest exercise in the world. Tiger came within hairlines of spilling at least four times. He has an acrobatic lust for climbing into awkward places. Also an acrobat's perfect coordination. But an insane lack of caution, part of which is compensated by his coordination, and part of which will someday bruise him in the wrong places if his luck gives out. May it hold. He's a good kid.

When we finished melting the wings clear the field was still closed in by the fog. Orenstein broke open a box he had brought from the morning's briefing and issued each of us a .45, a shoulder holster, an ammunition pouch, three clips, and a hunting knife. There were also two sets of binoculars—7 power Bausch and Lomb—one for the forward compartment and one for Tiger and me in the Blister compartment. We had a fine time strapping on the equipment and playing cowboys and Indians with our new toys. When the last redskin bit the

8

dust most of us took off for the civilian cafeteria for a second breakfast. The ramp was full of planes and their crews waiting to take off. Everyone was wearing knives and pistols. Just off the ramp we found a poster announcing that it was Armistice Day and that the field was open to civilians for the ceremonies. They were flocking into a specially built grandstand to watch us parade. It seemed suddenly very strange and dramatic and ironical to be issued knives and pistols and to be waiting to take off for war on Armistice day.

We had ham and eggs and coffee, and stopped by at the instrument shop to say goodbye to the Captain's girl (very nice) and finally made it back and the field finally cleared. We pulled the props through, ran up the engine and taxied out past the grandstand. Through the binoculars I could see the crowd cheering us. It made good colors—a thousand girls' hats and dresses—an autumn colored crowd.

But they cheered too soon. Taxiing out, the right strut went flat and we had to hobble back to pump it up and refill the hydraulic cylinder.

The next time out we made it. Take off was at 1108. Three more minutes would have been the exact ironic anniversary of a bad guess.

Nebraska was a good sight below us. The fields, perfectly patterned, were finishing the season—all cornstalks and tee-pees of sheaves. Nebraska seems to be corn where Kansas is wheat, otherwise there's little difference except that Nebraska seems a shade greener and that the light through broken clouds was right for a good picture. We climbed for altitude and were still climbing as we crossed and recrossed the Platte—slow, winding, wide, gun-metal colored and mottled everywhere with sandbars. A few minutes later we hit a solid undercast. I played casino with Blakely for a while (he owes me for two games at $5.00 a game). After a while I let him have my seat and I slept alongside the bomb-bay bulkhead.

We're going to Mather Field, California by way of a series

9

of doglegs to the south. We were originally briefed to go over the Rockies at Denver, but the weather forecast sent us south. I've never flown over the Rockies. I fell asleep regretting the mountains and Tiger woke me up shouting yippee and doing a St. Vitus clog. By radio compass, it developed, Army had scored four touchdowns against Notre Dame in the first quarter. Tiger seemed to have enough excitement to fill a stadium by himself. It's an American custom, I suppose, but so is sleep. There does seem to be a compromise.

I dozed for a while, woke, wrote that much somewhere over Texas and suddenly have my mountains. We're passing the Monzanto Mts. After these months of flying over Kansas, the Gulf of Mexico, and the southeast, mountains are a good sight.

LATER

There are times when all sorts of events come together with a startling lack of relationship. This is one of those times. We're flying over Arizona at 0200 (Central Time), the land below is a burnt titanic desert, we're heading for Tokio via Saipan, Smith is afraid of airsickness, ("A good crew chief belongs on the ground. If I'd wanted to fly, I'd've asked for it. I don't go for it.") and the radio and Tiger are all excitement over the Army-Notre Dame game. The announcer seems to think he's witnessing the history of an epoch, and I seem to think I'm waiting to watch a little history myself and we don't mean the same thing. And the radio command set just spoke up and ordered us to land at Kingman, Arizona, because of bad weather further west. And I'm thinking of the last—and only—time I was in Arizona. I drove from Boulder to Kingman in 1939, just after a cloud burst. The road had been scalloped out in great rushes of water. There were house-sized

10

chunks of macadam a hundred feet out in the desert. And there was a new Buick we found with its front wheels hanging in space over a 30-foot drop that had been road the day before.

Arizona seems to be that sort of a state—massive and elemental and not quite habitable. We're flying over a long stretch of burnt out wastelands. If my geology is anywhere near right this was a forest of volcanoes once. There are little hills of warm red stone with a cuplike hollow scattered everywhere below us—what a red clay angel cake might look like if left out in a hard rain and then baked by the sun. They're the last traces of old volcanoes unless I'm very wrong.

Right or wrong it's a weird planetary landscape—something the way the surface of the moon might look. A great sterile piling of rocks and weedless earth. It's a real catharsis and a good one—to see how endlessly the earth can waste itself. I find myself thinking of Robinson Jeffers. He's wrong, but it's just as unseeing to live a lifetime without ever being dwarfed by—by Arizona, I guess. That's as good a name as I know for it.

The Skipper just broke in on the intercom. The lower aft turret stowing indicator light is on meaning the turret's not in stowed position. I left Arizona just long enough to tell him it's all right, that the turret stows just a little off center, but won't interfere with his landing. But it reminds me that there's a terrific job to be done on the guns. As per Col. Causland's directive we were forbidden to go near our own plane while at Kearney. After three weeks of UAAF base unit care the lower aft and tail turrets are both messed up and all the guns are rusty. It's not that I dislike the Army—it just raises hell with my war effort.

We're coming into Kingman. The Skipper is having a wonderful time coming down from 19,000 in long beautiful banking dives. I just missed cracking my skull the first time the plane went out from under me.

11

Historical notes from a safety strap: Army has just outfootballed Notre Dame by 59-0 as per the most terrific barrage of language ever launched by a single announcer. In between spells of far from breathless excitement he has turned over all the record books as far back as Atalanta and the Golden Bulls to prove that there never was such an upset since Samson and Delilah.

As targets of opportunity he has also presented the radio announcer with selected aphorisms by every general from the Academy, all of whom (a) feel it to be a great day (b) talk through their noses (c) compared this football game with the "greater game being fought in the field of battle," (d) sending personal greetings to all the generals everywhere by name (and "their men"), (e) ended by saying "Carry on."

West Point seems badly in need of new blood in Public Speaking A. [Modern Language Association please note.]

NOVEMBER 11, 44—LATER
KINGMAN ARMY AIR FIELD

We landed just after 3 P.M. Kingman is a gunnery school buried away in a burnt bowl of the Walipi Mts. Beautiful to look at in a primordial way, but about as isolated as it's possible to be within the U.S.: The B-29's made a lot of excitement. While I was staring at the scattering of 25's, 26's, 39's, 63's, A-24's, AT-11's and Vulture Vibrators, a circle of saucer-eyed GI's and Johns were inching toward the 29's. For security reasons we are under orders to divulge no information—a larger assignment than I would have guessed. The Skipper left me to guard the ship until a base guard arrived and since no one knew my new .45 wasn't loaded, the badge of authority put something on my side, but I had a hard tussle to stay friendly and still leave all beans unspilled.

As soon as we landed the officers disappeared leaving the GI's to shift for themselves. I was all set to blast at the Skipper and to hell with consequences when he showed up a few hours later, locked up the ship, got a base guard put on it, and suddenly handed me a fifth of whiskey for the crew. I recognize apology when I meet it. I hope. I'm glad he made the gesture—partly for two good whiskey highballs, and more because a functioning crew needs to be a conscious unit. It's bad business for the pilot to walk out on his men. It's good business for mistakes to be acknowledged.

Signs in public places—from the Kingman Operations Room: (a) Large sign with arrow pointing to a door:

OFFICER'S LATRINE

(b) sign over door:

AUTHORIZED PERSONNEL
ON OFFICIAL BUSINESS
ONLY

KINGMAN, NOV. 12

Sunday afternoon. We woke at noon to discover the new local time made it 1000 o'clock. It's the best proof I've discovered to date that you can eat your cake and have it too. Sleep late and rise early. This best of all formidable worlds has its merits.

The field is still closed. There are terrific black clouds in the west, louring and immense.

Kingman is a school field, a miserable place in which to be stationed. All day men were marching by, double timing by, parading by. There are no lawns, but all the sand-and-gravel open spaces are lined by immaculately whitewashed stones and meticulously raked. All day I passed the terrific consumption of man hours that went for raking and whitewash-

13

ing. All very neat, but a hell of a job to give a man. If there's that much time to waste, let him read, gamble, fight, or get drunk, but why saddle any man with raking sand-lawns and white washing stones. It's where the training camps always go senseless.

There's a large cadet detachment here (gunnery—and post-transitional added pilot training as per the new extended training program.) Last night I watched the daily hour long retreat parade—white gloves, stiff attention, eyes front. All very pretty but my year in the cadets soured me for it. Something about a man standing at rigid attention for an hour—or just standing at rigid attention—riles my whatever it is feeling for whatever it is about human dignity. The retreat parade called it all back. That much "military ceremony" goes hand in hand with the stupidities of raked sand-lawns and white-washed stones.

And with a full guard-house, which I note. And with a list of 17 courtmartials which I further note listed on the bulletin board for the last week.

It's a well constructed field with good barracks, a tremendous mountain setting, and fair facilities, but it's in places like Kingman that war is really hell. There's not too much to be said for foxholes, I suspect, but sooner that than whitewashing stones.

The first snow of the season came down on the Mts. this afternoon. It's a good sight. Here in the bottom of the bowl the snow came down as hail and then changed to rain. It looks as though there may be more weather tomorrow.

The Skipper tells us we collect $7.00 per diem travel allowance from Kearney to destination. That's interesting.

It took us two tries to get out of KAAF. Two take-offs per departure seems to be our normal schedule. We got off once, circled over the tiny town of Kingman, and turned back and landed—just long enough for Smitty (Sydney Smith—Crew Chief) to whisper abracadabra into the No. 1 engine hood. They may even have done something mechanical, but if they did, it was faster than the eye. A few minutes later we were back in the air—this time for California.

Kingman to Mather is a short run—about 3 hours. A quick climb over the rest of Arizona, a hop over the Sierras, then North over Fresno to Sacramento and Mather Field.

The frosting was on the cake and the cake was cut and waiting from the minute we landed: trucks working to take us to quarters, officers running around through what was practically a guard of honor, and guards ready to take over the plane.

We ate unbelievably well. I quote the Mess Sgt. poised eagerly over a tray of Spanish olives, celery salad, and sweet pickles: "All we got ready is pork chops. Any you guys druther have lamb chops. I'll fry 'em up."

Fry two, Sgt. This is not the Army.

At supply we drew sheets (real sheets and plural) and were assigned to a spotless barracks with single cots. Not a two-decker in the place.

Best of all was the grass—green, thick and lush that surrounded the barracks everywhere that wasn't flower garden and flowering hedge. Smitty swore the grass looked good enough to eat, and to prove it he chewed a mouthful. My gesture was to pick a Nov. 13 tea-rose to stick in my flying cap. The lawns are studded with roses, peonies, and tropical looking plants. A solid bank of yard-high geraniums edges the barracks.

Naturally enough, I suppose, there was a lot of Chamber of Commerce horseplay. Saloz, Orenstein and Johnson are natives. Blakely is a semi-native. The four of them had such a high time demanding that we be impressed that I began to pray for rain. Even my rose was used against me. "Where else can you pick flowers in November." I had to point out that you can walk out and pick up a posey at any season right on Boston Common. Well, we were all being silly.

I'm fresh from a hot shower, powdered like a whore, and my bed has clean sheets (plural). The sequitur is obvious.

We brief and process again tomorrow. They must be in sad shape after a 3 weeks hands-off at Kearney.

NOV. 14, 1944
MATHER APOE

Our final processing today. Like all processings it repeated most of every other processing that ever was: a squint at our teeth, eyes, ears, and noses; a finger in the scrotum, a forced cough, and an O.K. for overseas duty. A short tussle with supply during which I wangled an illegal pair of sun-glasses for Smitty, and a semi-illegal GI wristwatch for myself. A lecture on emergency kits, tropical diseases, and venerealism. An exhortation by the chaplain. And roger, over, and out.

The medic hit one memorable definition: "If you have the trots, that's diarrhea. If the trots have you, that's dysentery."

The one other high was the Chaplain's contribution to Empire. "Remember in whatever lands you find yourself, you are Americans. Be proud of your religion and bear yourselves in such a way as to do credit to the fact that Americans are the world's guides and leaders." (Sic)

16

The Captains and the Kings depart, but there are still the Chaplains to carry the white man's burden.

And in the incidental course of things our stay at Kearney did for about $2500 worth of machine-gun barrels, pitted with rust. On orders of Col. Causland the ships were turned over to base personnel for maintenance, and crewmen were forbidden to work on the planes. The base didn't bother to touch the guns and in three weeks of wet weather the barrels dissolved away in rust. Our ship makes four coming in from Kearney needing an all around change in barrels. I suppose that's Army. We were anyway able to save the moving parts though we had a long session of scrubbing off rust.

Rumor is we leave tomorrow.

Rumor caught up with us at 3:30 and hauled us out of bed. The next thing to catch up with us was the Army: we spent four hours shivering on the ramp waiting to take off. We finally made it at 0803 on the first try.

We set out on sealed orders. To prevent foreknowledge of our final destination the courses are given out day by day. It would have been an excellent precaution if every one in the outfit hadn't known weeks ago that we're going to Saipan by way of Oahu and Kwajalein.

At 0827 we crossed San Francisco Bay and the Golden Gate Bridge and pointed out for Hawaii. The Golden Gate made a surprise picture—remote and tiny and a little bit like a boy's erector set left out on the lawn over night. Nonetheless we cleared it and it was very dramatic because we had all wanted it to be. To one side Alcatraz lay out in the morning sun looking very sunny and attractive. I suppose any number of house guests would think it attractive too—from 10,000 feet and heading away.

Once we had crossed the shore line we all sat back for the dramatic climax of seeing the last land go under the horizon. Except that it wasn't dramatic and it wasn't climactic: I'd had only about 3 hours sleep, all engines were running beautifully

17

beyond the need for watching for oil leaks, and the land took an interminable while to fade out. In fact I fell asleep on it, and goodbye to all the pre-notions I had of being moved by the last glimpse of America.

I'm ready to admit that I start silly, but I learn fast.

When I awoke we were riding an undercast that stayed solid almost the whole way. In glimpses through cracks in the clouds I got a total impression that there's a lot of water in the Pacific.

At 1406 the Captain opened the sealed orders. We land at John Rogers field on Oahu.

JOHN ROGERS FIELD
OAHU, NOV. 15, 44

We came in across Cocoanut Head, Diamond Head, and Waikiki. The Islands are an explorer's sight—you have a feeling nothing is impossible to those mountains. My glimpse of them was truncated by a band of clouds rolled out across the tops. I may never know how high they go. Unfinished, they seemed all the more possible. I've been wondering all evening what was hidden in the clouds.

John Rogers is a dusty sprawled out ATC strip. There are probably more landing strips in these Islands than in any five states back home. We drew our barracks and bedding, ate out of our mess kits, and sat down pretty well appalled at the prospect of nothing whatever to do. It seems a presage. We're only 10 hours from the states, but already I sense the possibilities of endless unbroken monotony.

All water on the Island has to be hauled in by truck from a purifying plant up in the hills. Each tent and hut has a water can. The trucks leave the water at a distribution point, and a man from each hut goes up to fill the can for the day.

Our distribution point is Rumor Park, site of the Saipan Post Office, the water barrels, four bushes, three benches, a Jap field piece, a Jap grove and odds and ends of Jap stonework. Rumor Park is as much an institution as a location or a sort of curb market for the rumor grapevine. More or less what the latrine was in training camp. It's where everyone comes at least once a day and where any story can be born.

Official Rumor Park box scores on yesterday's raid:

One hundred and four planes went out. Ninety-nine crossed the target. Five turned back for engine trouble. Four planes were lost—shot down and ditched at sea. One plane had to ditch in Tokio harbor. Another ditched about 75 miles out (The crew stand a good chance of being picked up by lifeguard subs.) Two were shot down over Japan. An unverified (and very large) number of planes burned out an engine apiece. Luckily no ship lost more than one engine.

The Rumor Park verdict is (a) that we went in too fast, (b) that things were pretty well snafu, (c) some good hits were made, (d) the next raid will be better.

The Rumor Park news bureau has it from unconfirmed sources that the 73rd Wing is up for Presidential Unit Citation for the raid, which has been classified as a Major Strike.

The news bureau also reports a Jap recon plane over the Island and Tinian yesterday. A Betty floated it yesterday afternoon and a Black Widow took off after him. Betty didn't have a chance. The Black Widow (P-61) did it in four minutes from take-off on the first pass.

I'm due on the line to take out our guns and check the CFC system.

LATER

The Island and the absence of women seem to be producing a fine crop of fantastic heads. Every man here seems to be in rebellion against hair. There are six schools: those that shave off everything, those that shave their heads and let their beards grow, those who let everything grow, the very few who stay normal, a good sprinkling that go in for experimental moustaches, and the lunatic fringe that raises fancy Van Dycks, billy goat whiskers, side burns or what have you. The final extremists are the Iroquois—those who shave their heads but leave a scalp lock.

There seems to be a fine abandon of getting away from it all. I suspect the whole male world is tired of business suits and haircuts à la standard. Or maybe it's the twelve-year-old in all of us. It couldn't happen if there were women around. I begin to suspect that without the female touch men enjoy their own ugliness.

Anyhow I'm growing my moustache again. I may as well confess now that Polly made me shave it off at Kearney.

Tiger, Chico, and Blakely (how could I forget) gave themselves cannonball haircuts a couple of days ago. A sad sight.

LATER

Mike O'Hara, just back from a critique of the mission, told me the story of one of the stupidest commands ever given.

It happened on yesterday's raid. There were only two

casualties on the planes that returned. One bombardier got a 20 mm in the leg. The other was a tail gunner—killed by 99 44/100% pure stupidity.

Heading home from the target the pilot called for an interphone check and couldn't raise an answer from the tail gunner sealed off in the tail pressurized compartment. After a few minutes the pilot decided the tail gunner must be wounded, *so he depressurized at 29,000 ft* and sent the radar man off to have a look. He found the tail gunner dead. The only thing wrong with him was a bump on the head—probably picked up when he keeled over from lack of oxygen. I suppose there will always be stupidity, but I wish there were some arrangement for stupidity to kill off the stupid instead of the innocent bystander. Score: one war department telegram. Cause: disconnected interphone and cockpit malfunction.

Last results of yesterday's raid: All 882nd ships back without a scratch. Some of the squadrons in the 500th Gr. picked up a little flack, but no casualties. Two planes were lost out of the 499th group. Levine's radio is out of order.

NOV. 26, '44

I seem to have done a fairly mangled job of putting down the tailgunner incident. What I get for writing when I'm sleepy. But badly told or not it's a sad story of a sad decision. People kept telling me about it all day.

For the rest it was a dull enough day. I cleaned guns all morning, puttered with the turrets, oil-stoned a lot of rust from the gun receivers, (I begin to see that this climate will leave me a lot of oil stoning to do), messed, read Ellery Queen's *Chinese Orange Mystery* (the only book in the hut), filled out a delayed gunnery report on the mission, messed, and went to briefing. The Squadron is up for Truk tomorrow, but our crew won't be going. The ground crew is still in process of changing #4 engine. It begins to appear that 27 will never get over a target, but I'll probably have other opinions on that soon enough.

Last and definitive returns from the Tokio raid are two planes lost. One ditched in Tokio harbor—after a collision with a Jap fighter—all hands unreported. The crew of the other came in today on a destroyer. Intelligence reports that within 30 minutes of the ditching in Tokio harbor an American sub was standing by within 10 miles to pick up survivors. It was no luck that time, but it's good to know that the air-sea rescue is keyed that high and that well.

I begin to be impatient for mail. Wonder when it will come through.

Levin, I discover, is a philosopher—Freshman year. He was full of philosophy seminars while I was trying to read Ellery Queen. With my private opinion that philosophy qua philosophy is 50% a hoax and 50% a legend unintelligibly stuck together by poets without sensuality or gift of language, the discussion stayed wild. Levin's all right. It's myself I'm not sure of. I seem to have a grudge against the motivating force of all philosophy—which seems to be to reduce everything to a single explanation. I really don't know enough but all the "philosophy" dished out to me at school was too close a cousin of theology. Neither, it seems to me, do well enough by the people on my block, who are usually very nice people when they aren't busy believing that God the Father is going to keep them in ectoplasm through eternity.

All my grudges ramble, I see. I think I'm reacting to the increase in local religion before a mission. There's something I just can't swallow about immortality. If I haven't been slightly drunk in Frisco inside a year from now, I will probably be very dead and wrapped in about as much soul as those caves full of Jap bones.

I see it's time to go to bed.

22

Piss-Call Charlie came over at midnight. Four Betty's sneaked in under the radar net by riding in on the wave tops. The radar works in a straight line, and—so I've been told—cannot pick up a warning below the horizon. Whether that, or someone asleep at the switch, or both, the radar muffed it and the Japs came in on a strafing run sounding their own warning—with machine guns.

I didn't even waken until it was practically over. The four planes highballed down the landing strip with their guns wide open. Then they peeled off and one buzzed over our area. (882nd.) I woke up when a burst of fifties cut loose about 3 inches over my head—I don't see how it could have been more than three inches. My cot is next to the screen door and the first thing I saw was a hosing of red tracers spurting past the door, and all the ground crew boys from the tents above us panicking past our huts to hide in the coral cliffs.

By whatever logic moves a waking mind I proceeded to spend at least five minutes groping for socks in the dark. When I finally got out the door the raid was over. There was a flare of light in the North Point, that I later discovered was a Betty burning. And another larger fire up on the ridge where the parking strips are—a 29 burning. The smoke went up in a huge smudge, thousands of feet into the moonlight, roiling black fumes highlighted on all the undersides of their contortions by the orange fire. Then it blew. I could feel the concussion all the way down the hill, a good two miles. The puff of fire went up at least two or three hundred feet, a great egg-shaped spurt of yellow, as I recall it, shot through by little silver sparkles. The Japs had caught it as the ground crews were gassing it up and when it blew bombs, gas tanks and gas truck went up together. It made a terrific saddening bier in the moonlight; somebody's ship that was through flying.

Then the Major (Major Wollcott) was calling for medics. Somebody in the tent area had caught a fifty—ours or theirs—in the last strafing run. It must have bounced; it went in his leg and out his hip. A nasty rip.

That's all I could learn, but it's a wonder more weren't hurt. The troops are panicky about raids and there's no air-raid discipline. Once the alarm is in it's every man for himself in a stampede for the cliffs. Coral is nothing to stumble and fall on. Nor is the path of that mob. The man who stumbles will need luck to come through whole.

I must have slept through the big scare. Either that, or I was too sleepy, or just too ignorant to get decently moved toward survival. Mostly ignorance I guess. No one had ever shot at me before, and I couldn't quite understand anyone beginning to. I went back to bed and saved my major discoveries for later.

In the morning the ships took off on schedule, except that the raid was in Tokio and not on Truk. It had been all along—my mistake. I spent the morning very domestically hauling and heating water for an immense accumulated laundry. One of those real bursts of energy that end with a great virtuous feeling of self satisfaction. I hung it all out in two lines, my head glowing with a 60 watt halo, smoked a cigarette for meritorious services, and went to chow where I expected hash and found roast beef, whereby I knew that virtue was not intended to go unrewarded in this best of all possible worlds.

I was halfway through the second of the three bites the Mess Sgt. had doled out to me when somebody shouted and the stampede began again with those who couldn't make it out the door stretched out under every available inch of planking. The Japs were back, this time with Zekes, and they were strafing. Two of them went overhead with their guns wide open and the colored engineers battalion on the hill was following them with batteries of fifties and ack-ack.

I couldn't see anything coming but I could hear it. I crouched by a window—wishful-thinking myself into believing that a half inch plank was some protection—but I never did see anything. The noise was terrific and too close and endless. Then it passed and we all raced for a look, but there was nothing to see. For all I know the clouds might have been barking at us. Except that there were more fires up on the line that meant more 29's burning on the ground.

The mess hall was a litter of abandoned mess kits and GI's appearing out of potato sacks and from under stoves and sinks. The smart boys I discovered later (by the time I got smart myself) were outside under the kitchen floor—a beautiful reinforced concrete never-to-be-sufficiently-praised kitchen floor.

Nobody had been hurt that I could see despite the terrific noise of machine guns close by. Nor were there any ambulances screaming in the distance. And since even the mess sgt. who usually doles out the meat in tiny chunks had lost interest in the roast beef, I reinforced my mess kit with a couple of choice slices and went back to eating.

The Jap was at least decent enough to let me finish the roast beef. I was down to the canned peaches when it began again. This time I made for the door, freezing en route behind a pile of crated canned goods while the blast went over. It's quite a sensation to be in love with a few crates of canned goods knowing damned well they can't stop a fifty and wondering whether or not you'll be full of caliber 50 holes the next second. As a crew member of a 29 I suppose I'm officially in the air raid business, but I can't say I enjoy learning it from the ground up.

The blast came so close I couldn't believe it would miss the mess hall, but it did. When it was over I made it outside through the officer's mess where I found Doc Grow and somebody's shavetail looking around with six eyes apiece while they held a piece of boiler plate ready for a shield.

They didn't have long to wait. I could see the Zeke banking over the parking area, and stood ready to duck if he came our way. He flattened out the bank with guns bearing dead on us. It was time to move and I did, but I was on the wrong side of the mess hall and there was no concrete floor. I jumped under the no-protection-whatever of the officers' mess and it all began again, but worse. I could see the fifties kicking up the ground to one side at a distance of what looked like 3/8 of an inch, but was probably about 20 yards. I remember wondering why he'd be strafing an empty field with a ripe weathered wooden mess hall a few yards to the left waiting for his incendiaries. The colored boys on the ridge were pouring a terrific barrage after him. He must have been hit before he reached the mess hall. I can't imagine anything else that would spoil his aim. The fires up in the parking area were proof enough that he knew his business.

Just as he got overhead the batteries on the ridge got him for good. There was a fluff of smoke, a few loose parts rattling on the roof, and he was gone. He crashed on the other side of the area in a litter of ruin.

Doc and I raced after him for a look, but there wasn't much to see. There were two patches of smoking plowed earth, one where he hit, and one where he bounced. Fuselage metal was scattered every way like crumpled tin foil. The engine had plowed down out of sight. One twisted prop blade lay on a pile of dirt, and one of his machine guns lay a few yards to one side—a solid bar of gun steel twisted into three snake arcs.

There were pieces of the pilot everywhere. His torso lay off to one side looking like a smokey roast. His head and both arms and legs were scattered around in the debris. The gunner that got him came racing down in a jeep and passed us before we reached the wreck. He had already cut off the parachute and was holding it as his private booty!

The ambulances were just racing off full of screams. The plane had hit just before a sand-bag revetement where a number of men had been hiding. The crash spurted burning gasoline on them and they ran in panic. The revetement was just on the edge of the coral cliffs and some of them jumped over and down forty feet to land on razor-sharp coral. It was grisly.

It went on all afternoon with breathers in between. The ships were out over Tokyo, but it was Jap day in Saipan. After the first raid an umbrella of P-47's and P-38's stayed up over the island, but they couldn't dog fight for fear of what stray bullets would do. On the third move ack-ack got four out of five zeroes. After that the PA system kept announcing new waves of Japs coming in and we watched the fighters go out to meet them and come back. Now and then a Zeke managed to get in. Then after a while the fighters started coming back alone. They must have dropped a lot of them at sea. But there are 7 B-29's burnt or burning and others damaged. A couple of B-24's from the 7th Air Force outfit here also burned. About 30 men from our outfit are killed or wounded. The servicing crews up on the line suffered most. One of the crew chiefs drove a tractor out in the middle of the strafing and towed his plane away from one that was burning. I like to think of our men doing things like that. It's good to have courage—nothing happens to the brave.

The planes are too crowded here. And the flights will soon be due back from Tokio. Orders just came through for all flyable planes to get off the ground and hole up in Guam. The planes back from the raid will meet us there. Strategic retreat. We leave in a few minutes.

NOV. 28, '44
GUAM—DEPOT FIELD

It's a short hop from Saipan to Guam—about an hour's flying time. We put down on a good macadam runway and were fed

27

in a huge empty hangar. With flourishes—free cigarettes, candy, gum, matches, tobacco, shaving cream. But still fried K rations in the mess kits. If I ever again eat stew or hash after this is over I'll need to be badly in love with whoever does the cooking.

After a while the planes back from the raid pulled in and we had a fine time comparing notes. No losses in the raid, no opposition whatever. The cowards who went to Tokio had it easy while we were sweating the second battle of Saipan.

We bunked in another hangar full of cots. There must have been 1500 cots in the hangar. It looked exactly like a stage set, one of the great proscenium doors opened on moonlight, clouds, and parked B-29's. The other opened on moonlight, clouds, and cocoanut trees. Under it all the rows of dark cots seemed to be waiting for a cue.

They got it soon enough. Things had hardly settled into sounds of breathing when a night shift of engineers came in stage right with two bulldozers, two graders, and any number of dump trucks and proceeded to work furiously at a road along the backside of the barracks. You've never slept until you've had a bulldozer in your bedroom. Some of the boys, exhausted from the raid, actually slept through it. The rest stirred on their cots but tried again. Doc and I gave up and went outside.

You couldn't have kept Doc down anyway. He gets a gleam in his eye at the sight of heavy construction equipment that a reasonable man would reserve for a beautiful woman. Orenstein can't be left on an airstrip for five minutes without acquiring a jeep. When Doc goes to work he flies by in at least a towing caterpillar. Once it was a steam roller. It wasn't five minutes before he was shoving boulders around with the bulldozer and lusting for the grader. I gave it up and went cocoanut hunting with a flashlight. I found any number of them, but after laborious husking every one turned up rotten. I discovered forever that there is no stench on earth that could last one round against a sour cocoanut. I had trouble holding my stomach. I also lost interest in cocoanuts for the time.

In a few minutes Doc and I and the engineers were fast friends. One of them was even ready to help me get good cocoanuts. It was the simplest thing in the world, he assured me—the good ones were up in the trees, all he had to do was knock over a few trees with the bulldozer and I'd have cocoanuts for the duration. I decided it wasn't worth it, but I wish now I'd let him: I'd like to be able to say I once picked cocoanuts in Guam with a bulldozer.

At ten o'clock the engineers knocked off for late chow and Doc and I went along. On the way one of the engineers went off for a few minutes and came back with a light socket. I had mentioned that I'd been trying to steal a light socket since I landed in Saipan. This one still had wires and a bulb in it and the bulb was still warm, but why look a gift socket in the bulb—I shall soon have a desk lamp. To top things off we had a spectacular meal—real fried eggs sunny side up, real ham (ham, not spam), good coffee, cake, bread, real butter—and ice water. There's ice on Guam. After spam, powdered eggs, and forever tepid water, not to mention tropical non-melt cheese-butter, the engineers mess made a feast fit for calendars. By the time we got back we were tired enough and well adjusted enough to sleep through bulldozers, graders, and all but the prop-wash of a late B-29 taxiing into the park. It turned its tail squarely into the hanger and blasted us all awake in a gale of noise and coral sand. An interested party could make a real study of artistic profanity under certain Army conditions: I wish I had a dictograph cylinder of that awakening.

The next morning settled down to being a nickle and dime poker game for the crew, but I passed it up to go exploring. I hopped a truck and rode a long way in some direction. After a while we passed a sign that read: GUAMANIAN REHABILITATION PROJECT. I suppose that makes the natives

Guamaniacs. The truck raced past a long row of jungle hovels full of indistinguishable natives, went on past the camp and ended up on a dead end at a QM depot. I obviously wasn't getting much exploring done. I hopped another truck and rode back. This time I was considerably surprised to spot a red-headed white woman in one of the native lean-to's. After enjoying my surprise the driver explained that the Navy had been to Guam. What a carrot top that gob must have been to undo all the Guamanian centuries of strictly asiatic hair at one swoop.

Guam I discover is much like Saipan except for denser vegetation, and a slightly more tropical look, probably the result of the cocoanut palms. We have practically none in Saipan.

Later in the morning Doc, Chico, and I set out to see the ruins of Agana. Agana is the principal city of Guam and still shows traces of having been—at least in spots—a truly elegant Spanish-looking town. The torn and truncated royal palms still line the quiet ruins of the plaza, and some of the stonework still stands, but the town was first shelled, then fought for from house to house. I doubt that there's a room in all of Agana that hasn't had a grenade tossed into it. Garapan in Saipan and Agana in Guam are the two most completely destroyed towns I've ever seen.

The natives have come back out of the hills and the Jap concentration camps—those who survived when the gentle Jap changed tactics from sweet to sullen just before losing the island. The natives patch the ruins as best they can and go back to what were their houses.

They're an alert and beautiful people with superb posture and bearing, intelligent faces, and good features. They are friendly, intelligent and amazingly cheerful with no docility whatever but what seemed to me a frank and self-appraising straightforwardness. They all speak English—many flawlessly—all the children go to American schools, and they think of themselves as Americans. America should be glad enough to have them. They have their own police, administrators, teachers, and civil affairs commissions, and they manage to fill the streets with amazingly attractive children. I liked what I saw. I liked the girls for being beautiful, and the boys for being lithe and straight and capable looking. And I liked all of them for knowing how to laugh. And it wasn't Sahib-grins they fed us. I talked to three or four of them, and I talked to marines who had been here since the island was taken. These people are real. I'm glad they have as perfect an island as Guam—it's still backward, but it's infinitely possible, and its greatest possibility is its people.

I went back again with Orenstein and Tiger in the afternoon and dug a couple of light sockets out of the ruins as replacement parts just in case. Orenstein took a picture of Tiger and me with a native policeman standing under the sign in front of police headquarters. A marine immediately arrested him for taking pictures without a permit. It took a little while but he talked himself out of it and all is well.

When we got back by way of the Navy PX (Lux and ink in hand—neither procurable in Saipan) we were alerted to take off. The Skipper had dug up two cases of COLD beer and it made pleasant waiting. When we finally moved out to take off Orenstein was missing. We waited around the ship until he finally drove up breathlessly a half an hour late—in a jeep. I'll never know what his uncanny knack is for finding jeeps.

We made it back to Saipan and the latest news—Charlie had been back for a little high altitude bombing. A half dozen Sallys this time. They did no damage and the ack-ack on Tinian (just across the straight) shot one down. They'll probably be over again tonight—there's a beautiful full moon.

31

Charlie hasn't shown up again. The last two days went in oilstoning rust from my guns and checking the system with Weinstein. Weinstein is the maintenance (groundcrew) CFC man assigned to the ship. A good man. He was a class behind me at Lowry. I suppose I once knew as much about the system as he did, but I've spent the last six months being a gunner while he was working in the guts of the system. I'm glad to have him around.

We were scheduled for another Tokio strike in the morning, and the two of us worked most of the last two days checking the system through. After it was all done and the guns were all loaded the raid was called off—weather over the target. We're supposed to unload the guns, but I'm trying to dodge it. We'll only have to load them again tomorrow.

The Jap raids have produced some unrecorded casualties. I was working on top of the ship most of yesterday afternoon. After a while I noticed a dim figure wearing full equipment (helmet, gas mask, belt, canteen, leggings, knife) hunched up by the door of the air raid sandbag shelter. He sat there unmoving all afternoon. It's a pitiable case of pure panic—he hasn't been out of his clothes or his equipment since the first strafing raid, and he won't get more than 10 yards from a shelter. He has a cache of K-rations up there. He just sits. It may of course be a stunt to get a psychiatrical discharge, but I doubt it. The privation of just sitting there is too much for anything but real mental upset. Someone that is in immediate charge of him has sense enough to leave him alone, but what he really needs is some competent psychiatry. And he should go back to the States. If only pragmatically he's certainly no good here—a weird, unwashed bundle of panic hugging the sandbags, and who knows what churns inside of him.

The other aftermath is a Major and a couple of lieutenants who have taken to living in the large coral caves—the caves where I found the dead Japs. They have it sandbagged, furnished and fixed for living as a super air raid shelter. A number of GI's have also taken to sleeping among the rocks. This afternoon Col. King called a meeting of all officers and rumor has it that he is about to issue orders that no GI's will live in the caves hereafter—there's not room enough for all the officers that need accommodation.

So to bed. Charlie didn't wake us last night. Maybe we'll get to sleep through this one.

FRIDAY, DEC. 1, '44

We had an alarm last night but no raid. I suspect the raids are due to fall off. According to cumulative reports all 13 planes that came over by daylight were shot down either here or at sea. The Japs have been scoring heavily, but all they know is that none of their planes returned. I hope that's good reasoning.

I was in the latrine this morning when some joker shouted "air-raid." He was promptly squelched, but it crossed my mind that probably the worst of all possible fates would be to be strafed on the stool. What an end paragraph that would be to anybody's human life.

I'm just back from breakfast where I note sublime signs of impending civilization from Saipan—real fried eggs—my first on the island. Ice is also impending. Via some fast talking by Orenstein that got us a triple A priority we have a refrigerator. At the moment our only power source is a part time captured Jap generator not reliable enough for refrigeration so the box stays in the 883rd mess hall pro tem. As soon as we get better power we'll have installed ice cubes. We also have a keg of coca-cola extract, two seltzer bottles, and a number of confiscated gas cartridges. Civilization impends.

It occurs to me that it takes a terrific lot of equipment to provide a single man in the field. I was casting a possessive eye over my traps and here's the quick inventory:

Flying equipment: Two helmets, one set of earphones, one throat-mike, one oxygen mask, one walk around bottle, one bail-out bottle, two cushions, one parachute, one first aid kit, one jungle survival kit, one emergency life raft (individual), one Mae West, one pair flying boots, one suit heavy flying clothes (pants and jacket), one pair sun glasses, one pair of goggles with a set of changeable lenses, one pair binoculars, one .45 pistol, 3 clips, 21 rounds, and shoulder holster, one field belt with canteen, hunting knife and small first aid kit, three pairs of gloves, one light flying suit, one flashlight, one CFC specialist's tool kit, 2 tool rolls for calibre 50's, one tool roll for 20 mms, one flak suit and helmet.

Field equipment: one gas mask, one dust respirator, one helmet and helmet liner, mosquito gloves and hand netting.

Clothing: three suntan pants, five suntan shirts, one OD pants and shirt, assorted caps, 16 cotton shorts, 18 undershirts, 7 towels, 21 pairs socks, a box full of handkerchiefs (Total includes official and semi-official issue). Two pairs of shoes, one pair clogs, one pair basketball shoes, raincoat, field jacket, fatigue leggings.

Local issue: one cot, one mosquito netting, one set of mosquito netting bars, one blanket, one bushel of dry pine needles under the blanket, one mattress cover, one roll of toilet paper, one gas decontamination outfit, one mess kit.

Baggage: one duffle bag, one barracks bag, one B-4 bag (aviator's suitcase pack), one A-3 bag (flying equipment carrier), one musette bag with various straps.

Unofficial issue: (variously acquired through diplomatic channels and petty larceny) incidental useful tools; one GI hack watch, navigation; 6 cans meat and vegetable stew; one aerosol bomb (self spraying—nothing to pump), extra flashlight, one table lamp (in construction), 20 feet of rope, one desk chair; cabinets and clothes racks (lumber pilfered), various airtight ammunition cans for preserving stamps, envelopes, odds and ends, one GI jackknife.

Odds and ends, one camera, one CFC tech order manual, 8 books, two ashtrays, one bottle of ink, one package of Lux, dog tags, one cocoanut, one pipe, one package pipe tobacco, two toilet article pouches, one can of coffee, an extra mess cup for boiling water, one B-17 airplane cushion, one bottle mosquito repellent, one packet official papers, two decks of cards, three dice, eight bottles of beer (two empty), one can grapefruit juice, two cans vegetable juice, three fountain pens, two automatic pencils, writing paper, one wallet, one can carbon tetrachloride, one can machine gun oil, one package sulfanilamide, pipe cleaners, foot powder, two dollars and thirty-four cents, one private broom, cigarettes, matches, two non-functioning cigarette lighters, one roll scotch tape, one roll friction tape, 3 spare light sockets, and one general litter.

Amazingly enough, I can give one or more good reasons for having everything but the nonfunctioning cigarette lighters. More relevantly I submit that Napoleon was wrong: an army gripes by its stomach, but it takes a lot more of just about everything to keep it travelling. Not that I'm any real criterion—as a gunner I'm one of the privileged class: I have leisure for pilfering, I have any amount of special issue, I have a permanent dry place in which to store things, I flew over in my own plane, master (more or less) of my own luggage. It's the boys in the foxholes that are sweating out this war. I'm part of the exclusive Saipan Hunt Club—hunting parties twice weekly (weather and mechanics permitting).

One of my teachers (Myron Files—Tufts) used to say that the best possible job for a writer was in the Fire Department—action in concentrated doses with long spells of musing leisure between. This life fits the requirement. I would like, though, to get over a target—even Tokio.

Well, maybe tomorrow.

The formula here is very simple: the B-29's take off from Saipan, fly over Tokio, drop their bombs, and return. The only trouble seems to be in getting started—everything could get started if only (a) the B-29's would get to take off from Saipan.

In the process of becoming a bitter old man I spent the morning unloading all the guns and undoing all the work I'll have to do over again at the last minute if we get to fly tomorrow. I refuse to be philosophical about it. Not that I'm in any great hurry to fly through flak; I'm fairly content to putter and wait. What irks me is spending one day getting things set and another getting them unset knowing that I'll have to reset them the next day. Nonetheless the Wing Orders demand the guns of parked planes be unloaded. That sounds sensible, but isn't. There's just no way of firing the guns accidentally.

Period.

Notes on Saipan ersatz and ingenuity collected at random:

(1) The 883rd seems to have a mechanical genius. Someone has built a wind operated washing machine. I saw the blades whirling in the distance and curiosity did the rest. When I got closer I found the revolving arms attached by a chain to a bicycle sprocket. The sprocket operated an eccentric arm made of wood that converted the circular motion of the blades to an up and down motion of a third arm running through a fixed guide. At the end of this last arm a plunger had been attached, and under it a tub full of dirty clothes. The wind blew, the sprocket flew, and splash splash the clothes were being pummeled free of dirt.

(2) How to get cold beer in Saipan (Shannon method). While unloading the guns I watched Shannon (assistant crew chief) pour out a bucket of 100 octane gas, toss in two cans of beer and then drop in an air hose. The gas bubbled away and was very soon evaporated leaving two heavily frosted cans of

beer. There wasn't even a trace of gasoline taste around the neck of the one I drank.

(3) A can of beer with the protruding top banged in and down makes a perfect ashtray. I see them everywhere.

(4) Sgt. Ciardi has his private electric light, adjustable via a swinging arm to the right shoulder of his easy chair or the right corner of his desk. Lights in the crew barracks go out at ten but stay on all night in the officers' quarters. I feel infinitely shrewd at having tapped my lamp into the officers' line.

(5) A no. 10 can properly hammered makes a fine lampshade.

(6) There seems to be quite a lot of necklace and bracelet making out of shells. Campbell bought a very attractive set for $20. I'd rather make my own.

(7) The powder from 8 shot gun or caliber 50 shells packed in a C ration can and detonated by a lit fuse will kill fish if (a) thrown where there are fish, (b) the fuse length is judged accurately. The medics warn against local fish but I'm still set on a fish fry.

Well.

Oh yes—we're due to go to Tokio tomorrow, but I know what I think.

DEC. 3, 1944

Inside the inside of a communique:

Official strike report, second attack wave: Target bombed—primary. Method of bombing—visual. Results—unobserved. Percentage of bomb hits within target area (1000 ft)—unobserved (Later waves reported large fires) Fighter apparition—heavy. Anti-aircraft fire—light, moderately accurate. Planes lost—one.

*　　　*　　　*

We were hauled out of bed at 4:30 on the morning of a long day. The lights in the Quonsett huts (we're still operating the lighting from a very limited bank of captured Jap generators with a total and only part time output of 25 watts) hadn't come on yet and we all looked a little ghastly dressing by flashlights.

After we had eaten we waited around for the trucks to take us to the line; stopped at Personal Equipment for parachutes, life rafts, oxygen equipment, and flak suits; and bounced on up to the ship to sweat out a rush job of loading the guns.

Things started poorly. To begin with we were a little late and Cordray was a little harassed. I refuse to work in a hurry at the CFC system—there are too many possibilities for error. The Skipper chose to cuss me out and I immediately, perhaps unwisely, made it clear that I don't like being cussed out. We crawled into the plane with a number of angers at work.

No. 3 engine immediately proceeded to spring a bad oil leak. We had to cut all engines and put Smitty (crew chief) to work on her. Meanwhile the other ships of our element were taxiing out ready to take off. At the last minute, Smitty shouted O.K., the ground crews pulled away the work stands, and we taxied out of our hardstand on the outside engines (#1, & #4) starting #2 and #3 as we moved down the taxi strip. We drew up on the runway, watched 24 (Plane #24) take off, and finally got our flag signal to go pounding the runway. Take off weight 142,000 lbs. That's a lot of weight to put into the air, and we were all sweating out the take-off run, but we got off the ground with a lot of runway to spare, though I had a feeling that we just cleared the trees at the end. It was 0746.

From there on to the target, we settled down to the forever long ocean run. We flew the first three hours at 500 ft. to burn off some gas before we started the climb. The Pacific was completely as always blank.

A short way out we test fired the turrets and I had just settled back into a self congratulatory mood as each gunner

38

reported All-Roger, when somebody noticed a jam on the outside right gun of the upper forward turret.

I dragged my tool kit out of the radar room and crawled down the tunnel on all fours for the fairly exhausting job of stripping the gun down in the air. In our system the guns are in pressure-sealed turrets. A man needs to be part eel to reach things inside. With luck, however, things went my way and I had it sweated clear sooner than I could have hoped. (The links had jammed in the link chutes, a round had jammed between the face of the bolt and the trunnion block, and the oil buffer had come out of adjustment.) I sealed the turret back and called T. J. (T. J. Moore—ringsight) to test. The Captain was sitting in the navigation hatch to check it, and I was watching the Captain. I heard the guns pounding inside the turret, and saw the Captain move. All O.K. You need to be as sweaty and exhausted as I was to know how beautiful a gesture can be.

When I got back to my station I found we had climbed to about 10,000. There was about 5/10ths of undercast below us. Through the cloud breaks the Pacific was an immense slate-blue floor strewn with the lint of whitecaps. They seem motionless from altitude. You have to watch an individual whitecap to see it move. Seen panoramically there is no motion—just the great stone floor of water and the blown wreckage of waves looking exactly like lint. Or perhaps feathers. Someone seems always to have just finished a terrific pillow fight.

And that's all there was until we sighted Japan. We crossed first a small volcanic island. I looked squarely down into the crater—a bowl like depression at the top of the bony mountain, and in the center of the bowl a great sheer shaft sinking out of sight. There was no activity left in it. A minute later we were over the coast near Tokio harbor.

At first it was all ours. The formation closed in tight and circled over the bay for the I. P. (Initial point of the bomb run). Just as we crossed the bay shore I saw the first flak—behind us at five o'clock and about 3000 ft too low. There must have been about two batteries there—keeping themselves busy but doing no good.

Doc was in the nose calling off landing fields below us and counting the planes, one hand on his bomb toggles, the other on his gun-sight. He didn't need to watch his bombsight—we dropped our bombs on the lead plane.

We were still on the bomb run when the fighters came in. About 70 of them—mostly Zekes, with a couple of Nicks and Irvings. I began to feel very busy and very useless. Tiger had control of the lower aft turret leaving me with a sight but no guns and there were Japs all over the sky. The bombs were hardly away when the first one barrelled through in a vertical bank winking his belly at me about two wing lengths away. I suddenly remembered somebody telling me that Zekes couldn't climb to 30,000. I wondered if the Zekes knew it. They not only had climbed to 30,000; judging from the air circus they put on they weren't even panting.

From there on it was a series of blurs and glimpses. Zekes were barrelling all through the formation every way but right side up. All the attacks our ship drew were from the nose—from 10 o'clock round to about 2 o'clock. Our ground speed was about 425 m.p.h. and the Zekes must have been doing as much or more from the opposite direction. That made our relative speeds something over 800 m.p.h. When the Zekes crossed us they went by fast.

I was cockeyed proud of the crew. Not a rattle in the bunch. The interphone clicked off the attacks easily and accurately. Every man was functioning calmly and well and it was a proud thing to know. This is the pilot's air corps, but it takes eleven men to fly a 29. And eleven men have to lose their fear and be sure of themselves before a crew can function. We functioned.

Left to right: "Doc" Crow, Bob Campbell, John Ciardi, Unknown, Unknown, "Tiger" Johnson, "Chico" Salez, "Frank" Franklin, "Mike" O'Hara, "Bud" Orenstein, "Mac" Cordray

Typical quarters area for non-air crew members (Saipan 1944–45)

View of bombardier's position
in B-29

John Ciardi receiving Air Medal from Brigadier General Emmett
(Rosie) O'Donnell (Easter 1945)

John Ciardi in flight suit

John Ciardi (second from right)
at crap table in Sergeant's Club (Saipan)

Checking upper forward turret on "Slick Dick"

Clouds over Japan from bombardier's position on B-29

American cemetery on Saipan

Saipan natives bathing

View of bombs leaving bomb bay of B-29

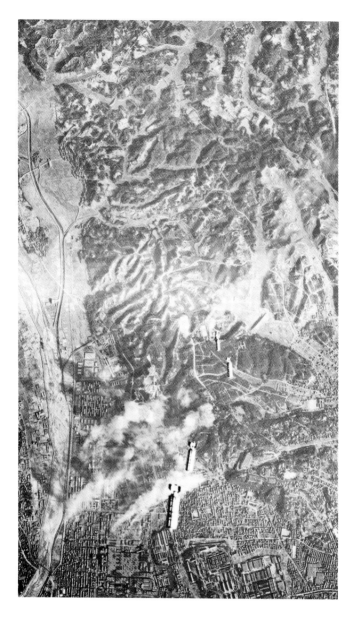

Factory in Mitsubishi, Japan (put out of commission after thirteen bombing missions)

Meanwhile the Zekes flashed by every which way and it was impossible to know exactly what was happening. Once I saw a flak burst—level and about 500 ft out. That was the only one I noticed. And once up ahead there was a puff of smoke and fire, and pieces of a Zeke's wreckage went floating past my window. With all the attacks from the nose, there was nothing to see from my blister but the break away and that was no more than a blur. Tiger and I were sharing the lower aft turret with Tiger in primary control. (The wing directive is that the CFC gunner will always occupy the side exercising secondary control in order to be free to leave his station and attend to malfunctions.) It's a ticklish business for two men to be using one turret in the heat of things, but we worked it, switching back and forth as we sighted attacks. As it happened none of the threatened attacks on my side came in. Tiger got a few quick bursts in, but I didn't fire a shot.

Up in the barber chair (ringsight) T. J. was having a busy time controlling the upper aft (two gun) and upper forward (four gun) turrets. In the nose Doc was spraying at planes all over the sky. One Zeke, I later discovered, tried to ram us. Doc put a first burst at him that made him veer off. He went past T. J. close enough to shake hands and scared hell out of Saloz by just missing the tail plane. T. J. put a 6-gun burst into him and the plane behind us reported him smoking as he went past, but we couldn't even claim a probable. Let's say a hopeful. Skipper has a quart reserved for the first man to score a confirmed fighter. It remains unclaimed.

Somewhere in the melee I looked out just in time to see our no. 1 ship (Z☐1) in trouble. Later reports put it down to a flak burst under the no. 3 engine. When I saw it no. 3 was feathered and no. 4 was burning badly. The whole formation slowed down trying to stay with her but it was no use. She lost altitude and speed rapidly, falling away from us. At about the same time Z☐7 had her nose wheel shot up by flak. I spotted it hanging down but she stayed with the formation. The Zekes were quick to spot trouble. First one then another broke off and dove at No. 1 for an easy kill. When I saw her last fighters were swarming all over her. (She never made it back: Later waves reported her wing crumpling and fighters all over her. Col. King and Col. Brugge were in her making what the boys call a CFC run. No. 7 made it back.).

Without any preamble we found ourselves out over the ocean again and clear of the fighters. I suddenly realized by my watch that we had been over Tokio almost 30 minutes and I hadn't so much as looked at the ground. There seemed to be more to look at in the sky. I crammed my head out the blister for a quick look and did get a one-two glimpse of Fujiyama, white-capped and cloudy. And that's as much as I've seen of Japan.

The mission was over—all but the long sweat back to base. Which means we still had a long way to go. About an hour out of Japan No. 4 engine began throwing vapor from the lower cylinders in front of the oil cooler. After a while I could see it wasn't vapor but oil spray. The sun was setting directly behind it, lighting up the spray and Blakely chose just that moment to stick his head out and cry "My god, we're on fire." That made pleasant reading over the interphone with about 1400 miles of Pacific still to go. I hushed him up none too gently and settled back to sweat it out. It threw oil for almost an hour and then stopped. I can't say I missed it.

And just then no. 3 began to throw sparks—the exhaust tube overheating. I stopped sweating no. 4 and settled down to keeping a hawk eye on 3—if it began to burn we wanted it feathered in a hurry. The sparks kept coming all the way in, but undangerously, and I managed to hold out, though it made good worrying.

Somewhere along the line (it had grown dark) Saloz reported he was freezing in the tail and we depressurized and went on oxygen to let him out. The B-29 has a weird heating

42

system. My feet were ice and three feet above me T. J. was sopping with sweat. Back in the tail Saloz was yelling and moaning about the cold and up in the nose it was so hot O'Hara was getting sick from it. When they couldn't stand turning loose any more heat we depressurized and I turned Saloz loose.

We'd no sooner gotten him in when I spotted two unidentified lights following us. It could have been ours, and it could have been a Jap with his lights reassuringly on. (We were only about 40 miles from the Jap-held Bonins.) We had to do it all over again to send Saloz back to the tail, and we turned on the CFC system just in time for Saloz to report his computer burned out. We never did find out what the lights were, and I have no complaints on that score with the tail computer DNIF.

I was having a terrific time keeping my eyes open to watch no. 3. I began to feel all over again that there's just too much water in the Pacific. It's a sort of gaudy extravagance. Oceans are all right as far as they go, but this one goes too far to be reasonable. We landed at 2110 (9:10) P.M. after 13 hrs and 35 minutes in the air.

There was still an Intelligence interrogation, a specialist's interrogation, and a medical check to get through. The medical check is the best one—it consists of drinking two ounces of whiskey. I was even too groggy to enjoy it. Orenstein offered us all drinks at the officer's Quonset—but we were tired enough to turn that down too. I didn't even eat.

One thing came out at the interrogation that I had been pretty sure of. The Zekes were fast and really did a big league job of throwing themselves around in fancy acrobatics, but not one of our planes came back with a bullet hole. The enormous relative speeds we were flying was part of it, but nevertheless we shot down about 2 dozen of them. What they really lacked was a plan of attack. Each plane was out solo, and all of them were so busy stunting they never did come to guns bearing. Nevertheless I doubt that they meant us any good. The interrogating officer always finishes his questioning by asking for general gripes. Tiger's was right on top: "Yeah—those guys were shooting at us."

Z□27 is now officially a veteran and may take a name for itself to go with the bomb painted on its side and labeled Tokio. All we need now is the right name and no one seems to have it. Just as long as the Japs don't have our number I don't care who has the name.

The day after. Slept late, lounged through the morning, spent all afternoon cleaning guns and picking at rust, and went to the movies in the evening. A Guy Named Joe. All about how to die in an airplane, but too noble. And there is no music up high. Just checks—check your switches, check reticle, check range knobs, sweat your engines, call attacks. It's the only way to come back, and it's what you do for one reason only—that wherever one race sets out to take over the rest for private exploitation somebody has to live crazily enough to stop it. It's not pretty. I resent the Hollywood touch in it. The Jap our guns shot down a few days ago is the way it ends: a piece of jaw here, an arm there, and a dismembered torso smoking like a charred roast. There aren't enough speeches or parades or posters in the world to make it pretty. There's not enough of anything in the world to justify it, except necessity. That this man set out to walk on another, and there'll be no world if he succeeds.

It's noon and the mess hall line is too long. I'll wait until after the first stampede.

Skipper called a meeting for this morning to name the ship—the pure democratic method: names were submitted and voted upon. Tiger and Blakely put in "Our Hope" T. J. was for "Isle Swan" Mike O'Hara—always the navigator— plugged "Heavenly Body." I suggested "Glamazon" but was more inclined toward "Thirty For Tonight" on the score that it would be some sort of distinction not to have a Petty Girl on the side of the ship.

Predictably, the Petty Girl won and the ship is now officially the "Heavenly Body." There are two bombs painted on her—we got credit for the first Tokio run.

The Skipper also reported that the Group is doing poorly. We've gone after the same target—one of the Nakashima engine plants—three times and reconaissance still shows it to be functioning. It seems to be lead trouble. Coming in in tight formation individual bomb runs are impossible—we'd be crashing into each other all over the sky. Therefore the squadron's bombs are dropped in unison when the lead ship drops its bombs. It hasn't worked too well so far. In fact we're scheduled for a soft mission next. We'll get combat credit, but it's practically a training mission, probably on the Bonins. We'll carry 20,000 lbs of bombs.

After the christening poll we all jeeped up to the ship to help the ground crew take out the bomb bay gas tanks to make room for bombs. The air raid siren went off while we were up there. I made for the gun emplacements to see the 40 mm's go into action, but nothing came over. The gun crews were squinting through their telescope sights watching two parachutes float down with P-38's flying rings around them. They were beyond range of the naked eye, but they showed up clearly in the sight. There seemed to be two stories: (a) the parachutes were Jap. (b) Two of ours collided in mid air. Considering the air raid they were probably Jap. I doubt that there'd be much chance to bail out of a P-38 after a collision.

It's probably time for chow.

Yesterday afternoon went in getting the guns and bomb racks ready for the raid. Of course it was postponed—that's routine by now. The PA system just announced another briefing for tonight.

Official information about those two parachutes puts them down as Jap. Our pea shooters intercepted a Jap photo-recon of a mysterious unidentified type and burned it down. Strangely enough the two parachutes were carrying boxes instead of personnel. That's all that was released. That and the fact that they fell out to sea.

We seem to have a new deal on the gun cleaning. A while back the rest of the GI's on the crew and I pointed out to the Captain that one of our reasons for joining a combat crew was laziness. As it got put: "We'd rather be shot at than work—if we wanted work we'd have joined a maintenance crew." All very brave and mot dramatique but a pure single entendre, meaning: root out some of the officers to clean the guns. The idea being that the guns keep all of us alive. Grow—to whose eternal credit be it said that he pays no attention whatever to rank—immediately pitched in and helped us, and knowing nothing about the guns just took orders and worked. It's a good man that doesn't need brass to make him feel whole and right. I can't always see eye to eye with him. He's basically the American go-getter and I'm basically not too sure the go is worth the getting, but I like him immensely for a sort of ruthless lack of all of my self assertion. He wants to be liked and he manages to win about 50% of the world over. The other 50% cordially loathe him as a clowning lout, but I'm in the 50% he wins over. He's a big, prevaricating, clowning, yarn-spinner with a boyish serious side and no notion at all that his tall yarns sometimes grow a bit incredible, but he has human warmth and a basic willingness to like people (which is an endless asset in any man)—and he's a damn good bombardier.

Skipper also assigned Orenstein to a share of the gun. Orenstein showed up very nattily with a Navy ensign, mentioned that he had been assigned the lower forward guns, showed the visiting ensign around and hasn't appeared since. It's fairly strange that I stay fond of him at times, but I do.

The big news that the PA system kept blatting all day yesterday and this morning was the meeting of all EM with the new Group Commander—Lt. Col. Dougherty, who is stepping into Col. King's place.

It was a pretty fair talk—all of it sounding very straight and above board. What sticks in my craw is that it was Dougherty who ordered five EM to bail out of a burning ship over Nebraska. He then proceeded to land with plane with all the officers intact. Two of the boys that jumped were killed. It's all in the chances of war I suppose, but the big thing is that the men were offered no choice.

Meanwhile, it was a straight from the shoulder get acquainted talk. We're invited to work hard and to present all gripes at least for discussion. The Col. promises us all he can get for us and he demands all we can give. That's all as it should be. I hope it turns out that way.

And it looks like the Bonins tomorrow.

Incident: It begins with Sgt. Ciardi racing down the road to-ward Headquarters at 8:40 to make an 8:30 briefing. The lights of a Jeep flared up and drew past.

Sgt. Ciardi: Hey, going up?

Voice: I'm just going to headquarters.

Sgt. Ciardi: Well, goddamn it, so am I. Let's go.

Business of climbing into jeep. Business of lights from a pass-ing truck lighting scene. Business of recognizing Col. Dough-erty. Elaborate business of not noticing.

The jeep pulled back into the friendly dark and stopped at headquarters where the Sgt. leaped out. Final business of keeping all pretenses current:

Sgt. Ciardi: Thanks, mac.

Silence.

Item: Bonins raid post-poned.

Item: Our travel time per diem is through the finance office. We were allowed seven dollars and something per day. But we forgot to subtract. The finance office did not.

Viz: Per diem allowance $7.00. Charges for quarters—$4.00 per day. Charges for meals—three per day at 75¢ per meal to eat K-ration hash.

This war is hell, but I hadn't realized it had become quite so total.

The anniversary of a bad guess started off with its own local celebration. Charlie (now expurgated to Bed-Check Charlie) came over at 4:00 A.M. The gun crews up on the line had been alerted for him, but something went wrong with the air-raid siren here on the shore; and for the second time I awoke to find a great flare from the line where a 29 was burning, the sky full of searchlights and tracers, and the barracks milling wildly.

I took the first strafing run lying on the floor with Levin. By now I begin to acquire my wits: it's sensible to hit the floor so as to provide a minimum target, but whereas the instinct seems to be to lie face down, one might as well hit it face up and see what happens. I lay there looking up and through the screening I saw the Jap go overhead at about 1000 ft. trailing fire. Seconds later there was a great flare at sea where he crashed.

The alert lasted quite a while. When I got to the air raid shelter we had built for the barracks, I found it crammed full with fugitives from other huts. I decided I might as well wander around.

Another Jap came in low from the East. The searchlights loomed their great impersonal fingers crisscrossing in the sky and caught and held him. Simultaneously the tracers began probing the intersection of the lights. They got him almost instantly. There was a sudden meteoric burst of light high in the sky and he dove straight into the ground, falling clearly visible against the background of his own flames to explode in a terrific explosion when he hit. The explosion was starred—like that of the 1st 29 I saw blow up in the last night raid—with small white spangles. Incendiary bombs I guess. The plane was 2-engined probably a Betty. We cheered as it fell. Strange what a difference it makes who rides the flame. Ours appall us, theirs we cheer. Inevitably I suppose, but it would harm nothing to kill with a last measure of pity.

After that two others went over high the searchlights following them across and flak breaking all around them, but neither were hit and soon after they had crossed I ducked under a barracks to have some cover against falling flak fragments. None fell near me, however, and nothing more seemed to happen. As always the action was glimpsed through confusion, a hide-and-seek through fairly heavy clouds. The PA system will probably announce the consolidated reports later.

LATER

I'm just back from a call to the orderly room. All crew members were P.A.'d in to sign a voluntary statement, viz.

(1) I, ... a crew member on a B-29 as . . . (crew position) . . . . agree to the use of my name in any Public Relations news releases from this theatre.

(2) I sign this statement willingly and with the foreknowledge of increased difficulties I may encounter if captured by the Jap due to my identity having been previously revealed to them.

NAME

RANK

SERIAL NO.

Hardly a purple patch in English literature but fairly self evident withal. It may very possibly result in somebody's suffering. I signed, but I wonder if releases of names at home is worth the potential difference. The trick of course is to keep coming back to base.

LATER

Three air raid alerts but nothing came over. In between I picked up some mail and found in it a $100 check from *Poetry Magazine* with notice of having been awarded the *Eunice Tietjens Memorial Prize* for 1944 for 3 poems in Nov. 43 and 7 poems in July '44. The prize is given this year for the first time. I like being the one to start it. Incidentally I discover

50

that a $100 check in Saipan is a useless piece of paper. I shall send it home.

Right after the third all clear we briefed for tomorrow, this time against Iwo Jima in the Bonins. Aside from posting the landing strips that have been breeding all our Bed-Check Charlie's (S-2's guess) there seems to be a massive combined operation that smells like invasion. First fighters go in and strafe, then we go over with 20,000 lbs of bombs apiece, then B-24's, then more strafing by Navy and Marine carrier based fighters, heavier strafing by B-25's, and finally shelling by a navy task force. It sounds like business, we get up at 3, and Charlie will probably break up what sleep there is. I'm going to bed.

Charlie didn't come over.

The day began at 0300 and proceeded to split itself very sharply two ways—most of the day went in our bond-selling tour to Iwo Jima, most of the night went in watching native dances.

Iwo Jima was a letdown. We ate, briefed, preflighted and were off by 0700, due over the target at 1000. We were flying through about 5/10's coverage of cumulus all the way and had pretty fair hopes of doing visual bombing. At 1002 we sighted the navy task force moving in—it seemed to be mostly cruisers—and simultaneously we saw the P-38's coming back from their strafing. We had watched 12 take off while we pre-flighted. We counted 12 going back. An element of 3 B-29's lead them and did the navigation. Wisely the 38's gave us a wide berth. Friend or foe it's not wise to point your nose at a bomber unless you mean to shoot it down. If your intentions are good you have no business in close.

At 1015 we were over Iwo Jima at 19,600 and flying over a 10/10th's undercast. The bombing had to be done by radar. The radar scope picked up the I. P. (initial point) unmistakeably. It was a large volcano and showed up perfectly on the scope. We radar-tracked the bomb run from there to the aiming point and let go: the bombardiers hit their switches and the bombs rained down. A terrific rain of bombs. Forty 500 pounders per plane. The top of the overcast was at 15,000 and we were at 19,600. As the last bombs cleared the bomb bays I noticed the first bombs disappear into the clouds—a 5000 ft. ladder of them hanging below each ship.

If the radar was anywhere near as accurate as it seemed to be Iwo Jima took a terrific pasting. We flew over in 10 plane waves. Each plane carried ten tons of bombs. There were eight waves. Between 1007 (first wave) and about 1030 (last wave) we dropped 800 tons of bombs. They disappeared into the clouds and it was over. No hits observed, no flak come up, no fighters were aloft.

The 24's went in after us with a few more gift packages. By then the cloud bank had split and they reported the whole island crater pocked. Adding together the P-38 once-over, our 800 tons, the B-24's, a few strafing B-25's, some carrier based raids, and a naval shelling to top it off, Iwo Jima had a busy day.

For us it was a milk run. On the way back we flew over an active volcano—just the smoking peak of it rising above the water, and that was all the land I saw. After Tokio, it was a welcome rest. We landed just before 1400 and were through interrogation about 1600.

The second part of the day began with a haircut after chow. Reynolds, ground CFC maintenance man, is the barber. My ground CFC man—Weinstein—is in the same barracks. After the haircut we all went to the 303rd group theatre to see a program of native dances.

It was my first real glimpse of the natives—not counting

glimpses through the wire of their restricted areas. There are two groups on the Island—Chamarras and Kanakas from the Carolines. Each group has a chief who came along and said something solemn in his native tongue over the PA system. Then the dancing began.

The "Carolinian Kanakas" (I quote the English-Jap-French-Spanish and native-tongue-speaking assistant chief) were by far the better dancers.

The Chamarras began with a dance for men and women. ("A man-woman dance.") An assorted group of boys—all about 16, and girls that seemed to range from 5 to 20 filed in and squatted. The only music was a chant with harmonica accompaniment. When the chant had gotten underway the five-year-old girl began to wiggle and a boy jumped out to join her, then an older girl, then another boy. Then, as the spirit moved them, new dancers jumped out, and, as the spirit moved them, those who had been dancing went back and squatted.

The costumes were a rare mixture. Everyone wore woven grass skirts, and most had some sort of a plaited grass headgear (some a band, some a crown effect, some a single belt of dried grass holding two or three spikes of grass erect on their heads.) Some were barefooted, but most—men and women—wore GI shoes. All the women wore cotton print dresses under their grass. The chiefs wore plain khaki shirts and pants, no grass, and did not dance. The men wore everything from blue jeans to loin cloths under their grass with most of them inclining to white or khaki GI drawers.

The second dance was by the Kanakas. An amazing performance. A column of fours about ten deep moved on stage. The dancers chanted the music, the harmonica player alternately played and chanted, and two callers shouted directions. One caller specialized in shouting "One-two-three marrrs" with a heavily trilled r all through each movement. As the movement ended the other caller—who seemed to be a sort of senior caller—shouted "Left-right, left-right, left-right.—

53

Tensah!" That seemed to end the movement. After a moment's pause the senior caller started it all again with a sharp quick shout of "Uh-oh!" After a few repetitions I discovered he was shouting "Once-more."

Whatever the native origins it didn't take long to discover that we were getting a dance version of something very obviously copied from marine drill. Like GI uniforms, native-police badges and harmonicas, the natives seem to be ready and very willing to incorporate the whole passing parade into their customs. I wonder if the dance will remain a standard one and what it will be saying say 50 years from now.

The individual movements themselves were each an intricate routine, each man changing his position in the formation several times while the formation remained intact. The whole thing full of intricate footwork, arm moving, hand clapping, and hip slapping. All but some of the more intricate footwork was fairly simple, but the sense of rhythm and synchronized timing was remarkable.

The third dance was a woman's dance. As they filed in you saw immediately that the women here are ugly compared to the men. Here, as in Guam, the men are lithe, muscular, alert, and attractive. On Guam the women were very often beautiful and beautifully poised. Here the women without exception are ugly, shapeless and fat—even the young ones. It became fairly obvious too, that it was all right to laugh at the women. The chiefs had sat in solemn dignity through the men's dance. When the women danced they laughed, jeered, and threw them advice. The women's dance was a dull half-motionless business of wiggles and waves. And to prove that there's a clown in every crowd, the show was stolen by a heavy bosomed come-on girl in the front row who beckoned on all the men in the audience and sneaked back after the dance was over for a solo round of buttock-wiggling in the international language.

The best dancing was in the stick dances. "The terrible war dance" said the assistant chief. Eighteen men came in lined up in two facing rows each carrying a hefty length of bamboo. Beginning slowly the sticks were tapped together in an intricate series of turns, ducks, and leaps. As the chant picked up speed the sticks thwanged harder and harder until a man needed complete assurance of the routine and complete agility to keep from being badly pounded on the skull. The dance was in several crescendo movements, each ending with a final increasingly violent thump of the sticks accompanied by a fierce shout. At the last thump two stout bamboo sticks shattered.

It seemed a long way from Iwo Jima and Tokio. And yet I had an assured feeling it was the same thing. All the difference I could see is that the Kanakas excite themselves before battle. We work to keep calm and the excitement hits afterwards. That I suppose is the essential difference between killing with a barbed stick and with dials and buttons. The war of the Chairs and the Cushions doesn't need a dance.

DEC. 13, '44

It's a fallacy to put calendars on these days. Time bunches and spreads—three or four days rush by at once and one day stretches forever. If ever there were timelessness we have it here. Even in the training camps there was the same featureless flow of days, but not as completely as here. There were passes and routines to punctuate things there. Here every day happens by itself, and the crews have no routine except to tend their guns and wait for a mission.

Most of the last few days went in reading and a couple of bouts of gun cleaning. The gun cleaning is automatic enough:

you start with a dirty gun and end with a clean one. The reading is less self-evident. I've read Hilton's *We Are Not Alone*, Steinbeck's *Cup of Gold*, something called *Dangerous Curves* by somebody named Chaney. Forester's *Beat to Quarters*, and one other I can't even remember full of detectives, stamp collectors and Ellery Queen pseudo-brilliance. I wonder where the books are that used to lift the top of my head, *Crime and Punishment* did. *Fathers and Children* did, *Mme. Bovary*, and *A Farewell to Arms*., and *The Grapes of Wrath* and *Strange Fruit* was close. There are others of course, but they fade. Say a dozen all told—with all the books that have been written there should have been more. There are too many professional story tellers and too few authors weaving their essential wish into a story that sings human.

Or maybe I'm bored. But I don't think I've ever been bored by the real thing.

In between times Skipper was brewing up a non-combat run to check one or two items such as air speed calibrating, turbo super-chargers, bomb releases, and the AFCE (automatic flight control equipment—the automatic pilot). He wangled permission to drop a few bombs on the Pagan Islands about 300 miles north of here, and everything was set to go including a full load of extra passengers (civilian technicians) until we arrived at the ship to find No. 1 engine torn down. No one had notified Smitty and he was busily hunting an oil leak.

The next day the Squadron took over and sent six planes—the four lead crews (Hurlbutt's, Van Trytes, La Marche's and ours) and two newly arrived crews (Schmidt's and one other.) We were all fairly well griped at the business of running a mission over enemy territory without getting combat credit. The Major was heartening—if you come back with any holes we'll give you credit for a mission.

We didn't pick up any holes but we did pick up a bad ten minutes when we sighted (a) an unidentified carrier, (b) thirty unidentified fighters. Since no 30 Japs ever turned from 6 B-29's, and since these gave us a miles-wide berth, we deduce *post facto* that they were friendly. Friendly or otherwise it's just as well they kept clear. We're all fairly trigger happy. We have to be. The assumption is that we're the easiest plane in the sky to identify and anyone coming too close does so deliberately and with no good intent.

The Pagans and the Volcano Islands are in a Northerly chain up from Saipan, a series of dead or dying volcano tops that just manage to lift above the water. Only the tallest peaks make it above the surface. It's fabulous to think what lies drowned there—the valleys and ranges, mountains that must be taller than the Rockies and never once touched except by the drowned.

Pagan Island is made up of two linked volcanoes, one dead and one in advanced dotage. Somebody has been dropping a lot of bombs there—the Jap landing strip is pockmarked with bomb craters. I suspect the Japs may even have abandoned it, though S-2 claims buildings still stand on the Island. It's hard to judge from 25,000'. We dropped half a dozen bombs on separate bombing runs and circled back home.

No opposition either way. The score to date:

Tokyo −   Tokyo +   Iwo Jima   Pagan±

Somewhere in the last few days time swallowed and disappeared. It began with one of those sudden chemical anxieties. Chemical because there was no rational part of me in it. We were put up for a mission to Nagoya and suddenly I dreaded it. It made a sleepless night and left me cursing mad in the morning and very glad to get under way. Once I was in the plane and touching the things that had to be done, the anxiety was over. I doubt that it will return. It takes a little time for me to get used to going to sleep at night knowing that I may be killed the next day. Ideally, I'd like to be unmoved by it, but I can't quite seem to manage it.

As it was the sleepless night would pass as a psychic premonition if I leaned toward psychic premonitions. We took off at 8:55, were almost over the target at 1500 and landed at 2205. In between we had trouble.

Nagoya is the third largest city of Japan with a population about that of San Francisco. Unlike Tokio, it is comparatively unmodernized and consequently highly inflammable. Also it has a Mitsubishi engine plant. The engine plant was our target.

We took off and test fired our guns while we jockeyed into formation. Immediately two of the four upper turret guns went out of action and I crawled forward to clean them. As always we flew the first few hours of gas off just above sea level then climbed for altitude when we were lighter. That gave me about four hours in which to have the turret opened before we pressurized.

It didn't do any good. The trouble was perfectly advertised in the raised gun covers. The cover cam was not bearing down on the extractor, and therefore not camming the round into the chamber. I had had the covers off the day before to clean them, and though theoretically they are interchangeable from gun to gun, two of them must have been switched and refused to stay latched under pressure. The wry pleasure of knowing it was my own fault was no help at all. The covers could not be changed in mid-air since they had to be worked on from above and outside. I tried uselessly for three hours to wire them down with odd scraps of wire, but they kept popping loose. Finally we had to climb. I sealed the turret for pressurization. Two guns is still a formidable turret, but that wasn't much help to think of either.

We finally crossed the coastline and saw Japan below us—a brown, wrinkled country. Geologically a new drowned coastline, much like the shores of Maine, except that Maine is green and unvolcanic. A hilly country that fell into the sea letting the water into the endless irregular network of valleys.

We had had lead-navigator trouble all the way and finally hit the coast about 80 miles off course. In the imperative name of SNAFU the formation went cruising about Japan for better than an hour looking for the target finally heading into Nagoya straight across the middle of a major air field we were carefully briefed to avoid.

The field was packed full of Frances's. Frances is the new twin-engine Jap fighter about which intelligence knew nothing except that it looked like a Mosquito. I don't know whether Intelligence knows any more about it now, but I know that it has a rate of climb. I watched the first two race down the runway and within seconds watched them climb to 15,000′. They came up on at least a 70° angle. And they kept coming.

No. 4 Engine picked just that moment to swallow a valve and break a rocker arm. The formation was still scouting around for Nagoya like clay pigeons in the teeth of a 100 knot headwind, and with No. 4 giving practically no power we couldn't keep up. By the time the Frances's had gotten between us and the formation it was time to clear out. We let our bombs go at a target of last resort, left the No. 4 prop windmilling to keep from advertising our trouble, and headed out for sea. A few miles out we were clear and had the prop feathered, but still had about 1/3 of the Pacific to limp across. Skipper called O'Hara for an ETA and was told 6 hrs. Then he called Campbell to find out how much gas we had and was told 4 hrs. and a half.

There wasn't much to do but sweat it out. As a last resort we could ditch but even if we landed on the water without cracking up, the Pacific is still no place to be in a rubber life raft. We began to lighten the ship. We depressurized and went on oxygen while we broke open the turrets and hauled out the ammunition to toss into the bomb bays. I was laboring at the belts like a stoker and changing walk-around bottles every 3 minutes. When I wasn't changing a bottle it hung from my shirt like an anchor getting in the way of every move. I finally tore it off and risked 20,000 feet without oxygen, but immediately went faint. The wind was whistling cold through the open turret but I sweated like a pig while the ammunition belts fell in coils around my feet until I was almost caught in my own trap. O'Hara, Franklin, and the radio and navigation equipment have to share one small compartment with the turret and the turret fills most of the space to start with. We had a fine half hour of getting in each other's way and I was limp with exhaustion when I finished and called T. J. to help me haul the belts through the turret.

We finally had the ammunition from the upper turret in the bomb bays. The belts in the lower turrets could be fired out and the links and cases would drop out. Doc salvoed the ammunition and our flak suits went with it for good measure. A while later Bob Campbell had the last gas out of the bomb bay tanks and we dropped those. They fell away trailing gasoline vapor and crashing into the radar dome on the way out, putting the radar spinner out of action.

There was nothing left to do but wait and sweat it out. O'Hara plotted a series of shrewd courses that would pick up favorable tail winds, and Skipper fondled the throttle settings to get the last bit of good out of the gas. And the Pacific stayed endlessly below.

Meanwhile the strike report came over. Good hits and large fires. No ships lost to enemy action. But the VHF was full of ship-to-ship distress. One of our crews—Grice's— had picked up some bad flak hits. It hit the water at 1700 and was lost. Some good boys went down in that one. Barry Campbell was a good red-head, and Kaufman had won a lot of my money by being a good gambler. That's a hell of an epitaph, but what good is an epitaph.

We kept getting VHF distress calls from other ships and sending out a few of our own. A second ship ditched at 1910. Later reports (next day) had them accounted for—picked up by a destroyer. Orenstein kept a log of his calls and position reports and probably was largely responsible for the rescue.

Meanwhile the Pacific stayed where it was and we stayed where we were—not in it. And eventually—Saipan. We called the tower for a straight in approach and they called back for us to land at Gardenia—the B-24 strip.

I thought I had really survived something until Joe Shannon (ground crew) came over in disgust. "Know how much gas you got?" I said it wasn't my department. Joe made a good Irish grimace of disgust and said "1400 gals! What's the matter with your engineer?"

A good question.

Pointedly however we're back and that will do till the next time.

Meanwhile the news is all guns and Doc Grow. Doc went on a moonlight requisitioning spree with colossal results. He borrowed a jeep, drove the jeep into a borrowed landing craft, piloted it over to Tinian, and came back with two 15×20 tarps, some lumber, 55 lbs of boneless choice merchant marine steak and a smoked ham. We had a steak fry last night that will do for some very long pleasant memories. And we're building a shack on the line with the tarps and lumber—a place to store guns.

Another mission goes over Nagoya tomorrow. Our crew won't be on it.

61

I'm reading Alexander Wolcott and he's clever, and almost real, and eventually dull. I'm also doing a lot of gun cleaning and with results: the CFC system is in perfect shape.

This afternoon we test-hopped the ship after repairs from the last Nagoya mission. In the course of throwing two stones at one bird the skipper checked Lt. Carrico out on a few last details of piloting the ship. Lt. Schmidt was lost with Capt. Grice on the last Nagoya raid and Schmidt's crew had no pilot for a while. Carrico was shifted from Squadron Operations Officer to a crew assignment and he was making up for a little too much desk time and not enough stick time. He did a good job and pulled a couple of top flight landings. Tomorrow night he takes his new crew on a night raid over Japan.

Ratings are Snafu and Blakely and Saloz are justifiably peeved. Skipper had them put in for Staff as of January 1. On the same list Tiger and T. J. go in for Corporal. I was left off because Blakely and Saloz have been in grade almost a year longer than me, and because I can and—I quote—will—end quote—make Tech according to the T. O. for CFC gunner. As it now develops Blakely and Saloz cannot make Staff on their present spec. numbers as Tail Gunner and Radar Operator. Their positions are frozen at Bush Sergeant despite their time in grade. Whereas I can in my position and probably will make Staff on the next list. It's fairly picayune to gripe about ratings, but even though I pick up another stripe from it, it's not a good situation. Blakely and Saloz are overdue for it. Come to that we're all overdue. The B-24 boys flying unopposed six-hour milk runs to the Bonins outrate us by about two stripes per man. Keeping the enlisted men underrated is as good a recipe for disaffection as any I know.

Why is the Army?

It was Nagoya again today, and we began by being bogged down. The Armament Section had loaded the upper left turret ammunition cans in backwards and we had to rip the turret open, haul out the cans and replace them properly before we could load the guns. Skipper was biting spikes and breathing fire. When Rudolph, the Armament Officer, drove up, Skipper threatened to Court Martial him. I begin to see the Skipper's pattern: he has the perfect ideal—efficiency. With a deep bow I admit and admire that he usually fulfills it himself. Sloppiness in a job sets him afire.

By the time the ammunition cans were straightened out we were already behind schedule. The rest of the formation was already in the air, but we had a chance of catching them. We turned on power and started the putt-putt (auxiliary generator) just in time to find the interphone dead. When we finally got a repairman and had the trouble patched it was too late to make our own formation—the 500th or Z□. We waited around for half an hour and took off with a later wave from the 497th A□ .

In the air all went well. We test fired the guns and all turrets checked out O.K. (Later we discovered only one gun in the lower forward turret had fired, but there's no way of telling in the air.) After the guns were checked out there was nothing to do for hours ahead. Tiger, T. J. and I settled back to catch up on sleep, waking up now and then to peek at the engines, all of which were running beautifully. About three hours out we were alerted to watch the sea for an A□ plane that had ditched after mechanical failure. I scanned the surface as conscientiously as I'd want someone else to scan for me in the same situation, feeling a bit peeved at Tiger and T. J. for going on dozing. After a while the VHF reported that the ship had been seen to bog down on an unsuccessful ditching. The 29's will float indefinitely after a successful ditching, but if they hit the water wrong they go down like stones. The sea was pretty rough, and the plane broke. It's another reminder that we live by accidents.

Over the target we had another reminder yet. The A☐ boys were running a badly messed up formation. We ran parallel to the coast a while and according to O'Hara missed our turn into the target. At that point the lead bombardier admitted he was messed up and we had to jockey the formation around for the deputy-leader to go into no. 1 position. (In a formation bomb-run only the lead bombardier sights. Flying wing-tip to wing-tip the bomb-sight can't be trusted to fly the plane for fear of collision. The lead plane goes over to the bombardier, the others fly formation on him, and all the other bombardiers toggle out their bombs when no. 1 drops his.).

It was there we had our close one. Two of them. The sky was full of fighters—Zekes (39′ single engine) and Irvings (55′ twin engine.) Going into the bomb run Doc called back "twin engine fighter direct at 2 o'clock." I threw the switches to take the lower forward turret and waited. T. J. had both upper turrets and was blasting away at a series of Irvings making head on attacks. Doc was waiting to toggle his bombs out. I set my reticle for 55 feet and caught the Irving just as he came round the wing. He came in at about 150 yds. I framed him beautifully, tracked him for a second or so and hit the trigger waiting for the plane to blow up. Nothing happened. The orange balls on his wing glared at me and four guns in his nose went past smoking, and my guns hadn't fired. The CFC department had wired the lower turret link ejection doors open to prevent a jam and at $-42°C$ the guns had frozen solid in the cold rush of air in the open doors. We had from forty to sixty separate attacks with only the two upper turrets and the tail working. I played out the rest of the act with blank cartridges. When a plane came in I turned the guns toward him, pressed the dead triggers and said, "Mene,

mene, tekel upharsin." It was a game I got very tired of very soon.

In the middle of it all we had another piece of sloppy formation flying and our own private miracle of minus 42. Doc toggled the bombs out on the lead bombardier and called for verification. I couldn't get my head into the blister to look out. The flak helmet wedged in the way. I ripped it off and looked out: no bombs. But cruising along 50 ft under our open bomb bay doors right down the bomb run was one of the A☐ boys doing a little sightseeing. Doc's warning lights were telling him no bombs had dropped and he was working the toggles hard. I interphoned a stop to that in a hurry. We were carrying 11 500-pounders with instantaneous fuses. If one of them had hit our little friend down below, both of us and a good piece of the nearest elements of the formation would have been making a badly splashed Christmas in and under Nagoya. The miracle was that our bomb releases had frozen tight.

The Skipper pulled us clear and we reopened the bomb bays. Doc tried to salvo but that stuck. Then he tried throwing the toggle off and on. After a few tries the releases broke through the freeze up and the bombs fell away—god knows where. There were lots of reminders on this trip.

Meanwhile there were orange balls all over the sky and one or two inaccurate boxes of flak. One of the boxes found a fighter, but he flew on through it with no visible damage. Chico was pumping away in the tail, and Doc was calling them out for T. J. who was running the six upper guns. I was still putting on my blank no cartridge stick-up routine, but T. J. was really logging them in. He hit at least four Irvings and one of them went by done for. Doc reported him smoking. Mike (O'Hara) had a glimpse of him going past the navigator's window throwing flames, and Chico saw him go into a spin belching fire and smoke.

As always, the attacks stopped at the coast. No planes lost to enemy action. Capt. Savage's ship was the day's closest. He went in with the formation we were scheduled for and missed, and he came out with two 20 mm HE holes alongside his astro-dome. One of the A□̂ ships in our formation had his stabilizer shot full of holes. Z□26 , Lt. Parson's ship, came home with a cal. 50 hole through no. 1 engine. We were unventilated and had all four engines.

We stayed at 25,000 a long way back to pick up some enormous tail winds at that level. As soon as we came down I test fired the lower turrets again. The low forward had loosened up and was firing out of one gun. The lower aft was still jammed.

On the ground I checked them and blew up. The lower forward had a gunner charger that had given out—unavoidable. But the lower aft was fouled up by (a) a cleaning patch left in the left gun, (b) a bent feed panel arm in the cover. The most elementary inspection should have caught that. The lower aft is Tiger's turret to service. When I called him on it he blew up in my face, and I blew back. He's a likable kid, but in no way Jap fighters will discount. This makes the third time he has been careless. He won't like it, but from here on I'm going to give his turret a pre-flight inspection of my own. Enemies have been made by less than that, but so have eleven dead men.

DEC. 23, '44

Guns had to be cleaned and replaced in a hurry. Carrico's crew is taking our ship on a milk run to Iwo Jima to pay Charlie a call. Lt. Col. Dougherty ran over Iwo Jima yesterday and found the air-strip repaired, ships on the line, and fighter opposition in the air. The squadron is sending out a security raid to nip Charlie in his rejuvenated bud. Too many 29's were lost on the ground while Charlie was having his own way. Incidentally he hasn't been back since our Iwo Jima—P-38, B-29, B-24, B-25, Navy shelling party.

The guns were all in and ready except Tiger's when it came time to quit. I finally found him in the sheet metal shop working on an "idea." How we stay friends gets to be a problem. He's up on the line now working on the guns in the dark.

I'm here muttering to myself.

DEC. 24, '44

I'm won a long way back to Tiger. He was working out a modification on the turret covers that really increases the accessibility to the guns. Now if only his guns will stay right.

DEC. 25, '44

Christmas had a short run on Saipan. It opened in the mess hall at noon with crepe-paper festoons, red paper bells, tinsel and a piled-on meal of ham, chicken, cranberry sauce, potatoes, sweet potatoes, pickles, peas, corn, bread, jam, fruit salad, coffee, tea, lemonade, apples and vitamin pills. After three bites I had mess kit hash—everything mixed into everything else and all the different sauces and juices mixed in together. Any way you look at it, it keeps life from growing complicated when you only have one dish. Also I discover that putting all your eggs in one basket produces omelettes. And all philosophy to one side, Christmas opened at 12 thirty for a short run.

The engagement went on through the afternoon, through, into, and beyond several fifths of bourbon that appeared from various stocks. The higher brass had us in for a couple of convivial fifths, and put us on our way with another to be divided among the unbrassed citizen-soldiers of the crew. We put that into commerative channels and had an hour or so of being fine and foolish till the liquor wore off and it was time for supper.

As soon as I got inside the mess hall I knew Christmas was over. Its dead body lay in a heap across the serving table: spam, cheese, crackers and synthetic lemonade. We held the wake quickly and without ceremony under the still surviving festoons of crepe-paper and the row of placards spelling out MERRY XMAS over the serving tables.

But the ghost stayed on. I had forgotten the Christmas party planned for the group theater. The main attraction was a highly advertised grapefruit punch into which 12 cases of gin were to be poured. So long as gin remained Christmas was not over. We all went.

The festivities began—as always—with a line. We formed three long queues (one for each squadron in the group, the 881st, 882nd, and 883rd) and held out our mess kits for the punch. Twelve cases waters down considerably when divided among 600 plus GI's but there was a hint of the right essence, and it came up ice-cold. The ice was something to celebrate in itself.

While we sweated out the line, the group brass took turns at pithy greetings over the PA system which gave out groans, grunts, bronx cheers, peeps, wheezes, growls, and finally a death rattle followed by absolute silence: it had gone dead.

The program called for 30 minutes of local talent from each squadron. Out of some perverse relish for the pointless I sat through the 881st squadrons opening 30 minutes and had quite a time of it watching "the quartette" (all the talent it seemed to have) cluster around a dead mike and swing, sway, and wiggle to the rhythm of a song that came stillborn out of the amplifier. It's fairly remarkable how meaningless gestures and postures can be when the recitation is pure silence. I had a feeling that there were four hopeless spastics on stage and that the flight surgeon should at least apply a sedative. Also I know now why silent movies always seem so silly to us. It isn't the flickering, it isn't even the posturing. It's simply that the whole thing disassociates and loses all relevance when the meaningful (or meaningless) noises that should accompany the gestures are scratched. I think I'll test it by stuffing cotton in my ears at the next talkie. My bet is that it will seem even sillier than Metro-Paramount-Universal meant it to be.

Strategically the PA system coughed twice and came back to life just as the 882nd came on with an orchestra, a trio, an imitator who played hot trumpet solos with only his vocal chords and his cupped hands, and T. J. Moore ("my boy") crooning heavily a la Sinatra. He did it enormously well.

And strategically again, Christmas went out and Charlie came in just as the 882nd squadron's program ended. It was a long alert. In the course of it a number of the boys got luridly stimulated raiding the remnants of the punch. And meanwhile 15 or 20 Betty's were cruising across the island with the searchlights following them and the flak popping around them but doing no good. At the height of things, while high flying Betty's drew the fire and attention a dive bomber sneaked in low and dropped a bomb square into one of the 29's parked on the line. Results as rumored and pretty well confirmed: one 29 instantly destroyed by the bomb hit, one very heavily damaged and probably destroyed, three heavily damaged, and eleven slightly damaged. Later another bomb was dropped in the harbor without damage. The gunners on the line shot down the dive-bomber too late. Things cleared then for a while. Then, far out to sea, three flares lit up the sky, hung a minute, and dove down faster and burning more fiercely than flares could. The Black Widows (P-61) had caught up with something. The three Japs burned out of the sky simultaneously.

We cheered. We always cheer. A few minutes later the all clear sounded, and "God bless us all" cried Tiny Tim.

Charlie must be coming from Truk this time. Iwo Jima is being too carefully neutralized to be usable.

We're in the full of the moon. Charlie's weather. As soon as the moon comes full the raids return. I had a loungy day, read Lion Feuchtwanger's *Power*, and then went to the 6:30 movie—*Our Hearts Were Young and Gay.* Just as THE END flashed on the screen, the siren went off. Perfect timing.

The radar had picked Charlie up a long way out. After a long while no. 1 Charlie came over high and in the search-lights dodging in and out of the clouds through a terrific flak barrage, but he got away.

After he left things quieted down. Doc and I stretched out on the sandbags of the shelter and watched the moon race in and out of the clouds. There was a terrific shifty wind blowing up there. The stars whistled down the cloud gaps like late traffic across an intersection and the moon came on and off like a spotlight, bright and just a hair short of full, as the clouds reeled past below it. It seemed, as always, incredible that it was the clouds that were racing and the moon that was marking time. All that the senses know is that nothing but fairy tales ever come true, and the moon was racing across the motionless clouds, while behind it the constellations rushed in and out of the cloud domes like coded ticker-tape flowing out of an endless machine.

The raid was beautifully nipped and no bombs were dropped. Doc and I sat together under the loudspeaker eaves-dropping on the island warning net from "Condor base"

(Saipan) to the nightfighters that were out to intercept "the bogies" before they got here.

The talk was all in self evident code. The radar man called off targets, bearings, and courses to the fighters: "Condor base, target two-seven, one-two-zero miles, angels one-five, bearing three-three-zero degrees, course one-eight-zero. One bogey. Condor out." (Saipan central: target 27, 120 miles, 1500 ft, bearing from island 330° on a course of 180°. One enemy plane. End transmission.)

A number of targets were being tracked simultaneously. One came within 20 miles and in the Northeast we saw a sudden star glow in the sky and dive. A minute later the loud-speaker was back to scratch the target: "Condor base, target 3 has been shot down by Charwoman." "Charwoman" is the nightfighter, in this case the Black Widow (P-61).

After the Charwomen left their third cinder in the sky, the loudspeaker crackled one last alert "To all gun control—condition is green" (Green = alert, white = clear, red = attack.) Then a minute later "Condor base to all gun control condition is now white. Condor over and out." The sirens swirled out the all clear and it was over, but we'll probably be wailed out of bed again before morning.

And to prove that the world is—at least 50% of the time—an accidental juxtaposition of irrelevancies, two letters received in today's mail, the first one a pencilled scrawl on a sheet of notepaper engraved with a horse, a Greek cavalry-man, and the single word TROJAN, the second on USO stationery and containing a self-addressed envelope.

1

XXX W XXth St.
Los Angeles, Calif.
Nov. 26. '1944

Dear Mr. Ciardi:

Please send me information regarding your poetry. I am interested in knowing whether or not you have published, where, and how

I could obtain copies of your poetry. I have read and enjoyed your recent poetry in "*Poetry*" Magazine, and would like to know your opinion on new poetry and the possibilities of new writers and their future, I would appreciate copies of your poetry, and possibilities of marketing and selling for an "embryo" poet.

Thanking you sincerely,
Miss Barbara [Illegible]

No. 2

11/26/44

Cpl. John Ciardi
Medford, Massachusetts
Dear Cpl. Ciardi,

I was reading this month's Poetry at the S. Carolina University library this afternoon, and not having had enough of your work there, dug into the files and found some more poems in a July '44 issue and one before that, I think. . . . I remember only an image here and there, and casual reading of poetry leaves only a fragrant taste (if it is good poetry), and I'm sure it was, and so I write you as an admirer and as an autograph collector. I'd like very much to add some bit of your manuscript to my collection of modern poetry ms., and would appreciate anything you send me. A wooden request, but not from a wooden motive! One day I hope to give my collection to my college and there some bit of your ms. may have a longer life than it might otherwise have had.

I admire your working on in the face of barracks monastery, and the terrible boredom that certainly must threaten any creative work. I admire so much the courage and the perception it requires to cut the fog of this life—to poetry. It seems almost impossible.

I hope you will think my request a sincere one. If you can, I can place your ms. on an album page opposite any writer you wish—except Melville and Emily Dickinson. My pocket book and the demand makes them impossible. In English literature Leigh Hunt is my earliest, I think.

I hope this reaches you with so vague an address. Thank you.

Sincerely,
Cpl. T. B. Nomatter.

11: 15 P.M. I'm burning the midnight dry-cell.

It was a fairly purposeless day—slept late, did nothing. A V-mail from Gin in the afternoon, a Bob Crosby film after supper.

I did finish Lion Feuchtwanger's *Power* during the day. Aside from the great granite crags of not quite English prose that seem to strew the aftermath of all translations from the German, it could have been a much more impressive thing for me could I have whipped up a little more enthusiasm for the author. There are some fine touches, and a carefully worked out plot. Strangely, I have a feeling that the Duchess, incidental to the plot, and the Duke, a caricature, are the only really understandable people in the book. The Duchess somehow comes out real (as well as useless.)

For the rest I grow out of sympathy with the windy transcendentalism of the gnomic mind. I think I know my disagreement. When one sort of man needs the answer to a question he sits down and tries to meditate it out of himself. When another sort of man needs an answer he goes out of himself and looks for the data of known fact with which to piece an answer. Feuchtwanger is a meditator. There's too much of Warfel's "To the inexplicable in us and above us." Or it's like Robinson Jeffers going out to look at a stone until he gets tuned back to cosmic harmony. Or like Leibnitz setting out to meditate out of himself the nature of everything in general (what used to be called philosophy) and ending up with a wild row of monads.

It's a poor method. I'm alien to it. I prefer the second. I suppose it would have to be called the scientific method. I'd almost say the rational method, but it suggests too much scholastic logic. Most men, great and small and all other sizes, could do with a lot less deducing and a lot more looking and seeing.

73

Sooner or later, I suppose, you have to do some logical guessing, but it can afford to wait till it's unavoidable. What good is a syllogism on 2 + 2. And what good is a mystification of sainthood out of guesswork when psychology can already tell us more about religion than all the testaments put together.

Finally I suppose I dislike most facing a book full of characters out of this world toward the nebulae of immortality. I'd rather have them here where I begin to see my way around.

Well.

After dark, Doc and I made a military adjustment for a jeep and drove around surveying. We surveyed a couple of metal packing cases into the jeep and now have foot lockers. On the way (I was driving) Doc turned me off the road and through byways into a rut between two towering earth banks. It went on for miles. Halfway through it when I was already beginning to think we had driven into a cave, Doc volunteered the information that we were up on the hill in Jap country. It was fairly amazing how every post began to look like a wandering Jap, and every shadow seemed to outline a sniper. Next time I want to know where we're going before we start.

Van Trite's crew took off for a night recon over Japan (alone) and hasn't come back. They carried Lt. Col. Dougherty as X. Our ship—27—is on the red cross until new blisters arrive. My blister has a burr, Tiger's has six cracks. At first they wouldn't ground us because no replacements are available for blisters. Eventually someone recognized that we were only flying along till the blister blew, probably killing Tiger. We haven't flown for a week or better.

LATER

The word is Van Trite ditched about 130 miles north of here. Lt. Colonel Brannock flew over them. The report is that 8 out of the 12 survived.

All crewmen reported alive and on a small island awaiting a destroyer to pick them up.

I slept late, went up to the line for a ditching drill (coincidental but non seq on Van Trite's ditching—it had been scheduled several days ago).

Van Trite's boys are back. All OK except for the navigator who broke his leg. The ship split in two. The tail floated for about 30 minutes. The forward section was still afloat when they were rescued. The ship split just aft of the ring sight and just forward of the upper aft turret. Immediately on impact it filled with several feet of water. The B-29 incidentally is one of the few land aircraft that will float (sometimes) when properly ditched. One that ditched sometime back in the Bay of Bengal floated for three days until a destroyer sank it with gunfire. In comparison a B-17 will stay afloat from 30–90 seconds only.

The boys are fairly well soured at Lt. Col. Dougherty. The report is that Dougherty (wing commander) kept them over Japan looking for a good target of opportunity an hour and a quarter longer than the navigator's estimated time of return and the flight engineer's gas consumption curve permitted. As a result they ran out of gas on the way back and had to ditch. Total: one navigator's leg, one crew unnecessarily risked, one B-29 forming barnacles.

I seem to see a lot of stupidity these days.

A while back one of the officers, caught up in everybody's game of when-do-we-get-to-go-home, gave the outfit a slogan: "The Golden Gate in '48." It could be too right, but we need something a bit closer. I make my slogan: "Stay alive in '45." All things considered, I can't see any other real impediment to fulfilling a beautiful age.

And the slogan will have to be my total contribution to right-living and high-thinking. I embark with no resolutions. It's too late anyhow. I broke all the possible resolutions last night.

The whiskey caches around the area began emerging about supper time. A couple of the boys in the Quonsett were fairly well spiked by six-thirty or so. At seven o'clock we had a false-alarm air-raid—probably part of somebody's celebration—and I went out into the field between our Quonsetts and the officers' Quonsetts (BGQ for Bachelor Gunners' Quarters and BOQ for Bachelor Officers' Quarters). Bud Orenstein was bumping around there in the dark with a naval Ensign, Hank Mannheim, an old pal who had popped in off a cruiser. There were loud and bacchic noises coming from the darkened BOQ, and after a while we gave up the raid and all went inside.

The Quonsett quartered our officers and those on Carrico's (formerly Schmidt's) crew. They had done well by themselves. There were glasses, an endless row of canned fruit juices, eight empty fifths of Schenleys, and—miraculously—two twenty gallon mess hall pots full of chipped ice. Opportunity is opportunity: I went about the serious business of getting drunk.

Bud, Hank, and I were still on the fastidious side of sobriety. When Bob Campbell began throwing glasses and coke bottles down the length of the barracks we decided to sit out on the porch. It wasn't really the glasses we objected to. Bob was still sober enough to throw them away from the crowd. Bud phrased the real objection. "Throw all the damn glasses you want, but when it gets so noisy you can't hear them break—make mine fresh air."

We sat on the porch and talked about which city had the most easily accessible women. We decided on Kansas City. Then one of the officers from one of the other crews came out and asked if I hadn't gone to Michigan, and it turned out we had been in different grad schools at the same time so we sat and talked Michigan through five stiff whiskies and water and without much transition we were all inside singing what bawdy songs we knew and singing them all very badly and too noisily while Bob hunted around for glasses to smash and Doc Grow sat off by himself looking very owl-eyed and red faced and 120% a-grin at nothing in particular. The empty bottles had about doubled, and the spare glasses had about disappeared. I put mine down for a minute—a mistake I realized immediately—and before my hand was six inches away from it Bob had picked it up and sent it sailing. It seemed to be a personal campaign against empty glasses. An empty glass was a fifth columnist in the party and had to be weeded out. I suggested filling them instead of smashing them and it seemed to start a whole new train of possibility, but Bob finally put it aside with a gloomy shake of the head and a verdict that war was hell.

Meanwhile Hank had heard rumors of a couple of nurses at the officers club. White women! He insisted Orenstein take him over, and I was insisted along. Orenstein dug out a fresh fifth and handed it to me in place of my defunct glass. From there on I drank out of the bottle.

Outside we ran into a few important delays. I don't remember what they were about but things had to be discussed. All at once somebody down by the shore cut loose with a tommy gun. Almost everybody had his piece with him because of the false alarm alert. In no time at all pistols and carbines were popping off all over the area. I looked at my watch—midnight. All at once the batteries of fifties up on the hill let go, firing out to sea. The tracers zoomed above our heads all over the sky.

Somehow by the time we reached the club my fifth was down to its last gurgles. All the lights were out and there were no nurses. We sat out on the ledge and watched the waves wash in below us and I finished the fifth. For no reason at all a character named Lt. Gibbs came by and Bud did the introductions. I was introduced as Major Ciardi of the Marines because we already had the Army and Navy and because the Marines wear no shoulder straps on suntans. Lt. Gibbs I soon recognized as a favorite pest from Walker Field. He was then Athletic Director. At present he seems to be Custodian of the Officers Whiskey Fund and Supervisor of the Club.

The good Lt. was a bit doubtful of my rank. He threw a flashlight around, saw no insignia and began.

"Major, will you tell me why you don't wear insignia."

"Captain Gibbs?"

"Lt. Gibbs, if you please. About your insignia."

"But Capt. Gibbs, allow me to say, pleases me better. If you please."

"Will you tell me, Major, why you wear no insignia."

"I sent my shirt to the laundry and it came back frayed, Capt."

"May I see your A.G.O. pass."

"Ah. I sent my wallet into a crap game and it came back in tatters."

"You mean to say you have no identification, Major."

"May I suggest fingerprints, Capt."

Meanwhile Bud and Hank had gone into what was obviously a longer practiced routine. They placed themselves between the Gibbs character and me and carried on a breathless argument with enormous gestures and loud double talk while

78

I kept the Gibbs at partial bay, while we all edged toward the door.

Bud was being the interlocutor and Hank was being Mr. Bones. Part of it went:

"Hank why does the navy weigh anchor?"

"That's to keep track of corrosion. After it loses a certain percentage of weight it goes back for replating."

"Well what about hissing waves. Why are they angry?"

"Because they requested overseas service and can't get it. It makes them mean."

"I get it: mean sea level."

There was an endless machine-gun flow of it. When we reached the door Bud shouted, "One two three, the Hell with Gibbs," and ran off into the trees feeling immensely pleased.

By that time there was trouble abroad. Shots were being fired all over the area, and those sane enough or sober enough or both were already in the air-raid sandbag shelters. Major Wollcott, Ground C.O., pretty well in whiskey himself was going through the frantic motions of trying to restore order. As we passed him, he was having a call sent out for all Master Sgts. to report to the orderly room. I sensed a grievance and decided to picket. A this-squadron-is-unfair-to-buck-sgts. motif. Why couldn't buck sgts. report to the orderly room. The Major's trigger finger was hot. He turned to Bud.

"Lt. arrest that man."

Bud: "Sir? Yessir. What charges do you wish to prefer?"

Major: "Charges? Oh, charges. Well—"

Voice: "Insubordination."

Major: "That's right: insubordination. That's a good charge."

With drunken irrelevancy he came racing over to me. "Ciardi, if I didn't know you were such a slept-with good fellow, I'd have you arrested. Go to bed. You're drunk."

"Yessir. Happy New Year sir."

"Hey. Did you fire your pistol?"

"Want to smell it, sir?" I held it out to him and he made violent gestures of pointing it six other ways. He didn't smell it. "Get the hell to bed," he said.

I'd gone about 10 paces when the PA system screamed out. "Sgt. Ciardi report to Lt. Col. Dougherty at 9:00 tomorrow morning."

Somewhere I left Bud and Hank, and somewhere there was a blare of speakers ordering everyone to turn in firearms, and somewhere I flopped on some sandbags and fell asleep because the line was too long, and somewhere somebody turned in my .45 and then woke me up and told me to go to bed.

I was considerably surprised to wake up at 7:00 A.M. feeling fine and healthy and ravishing for breakfast.

At 9:00 I reported to the Col. at Group Headquarters. He wasn't in and there was a grim air in his wake. Somebody was due to suffer for last night's wild shooting. While I waited the Orderly Room called. I was told not to see the Col. but report to Major Wollcott instead.

He was waiting for me on the porch of his quarters, wearing evident signs that he hadn't slept off his liquor too well.

"Ciardi," he said, "did you see the Colonel?"

"No sir."

"That's good, that's good. Just forget it will you? I was a little—well, forget it, will you?"

The moral being that you can't arrest a man without charges. The Major would have had trouble sending the Col. a report. It was a strange situation, but liquor makes strangers of us all. The Major is a good man for my money.

"All forgotten, sir," I said.

"Swell."

I turned to go.

"Happy New Year, Ciardi," he said.

"Happy New Year to you, sir."

We shall see. Meanwhile: Stay Alive in '45.

Things happen. I sit here this morning waiting for Sully (Sgt. Sullivan) to pick me up in a jeep to go visit Levin in the hospital. It's a long story, and it's a good day, the kind of day I'd like it to be forever, the kind of day when I know where I am and think I can see where I'm going. One of the places I could be going is a rocky mountain side in Japan, or the bottom of the Pacific. That's a matter of percentages. The other place will be home, and I know which bed, and an endless number of clean pages to fill with the right words about the right kind of seeing. The mountain side and the bottom of the Pacific are darker and nearer today than I like to think about, but it's a good day for being alive, and it's good to know the divisions accurately. It's good even to know that I'm afraid to die. It's one more thing known on a day when I feel as if I've found out a lot of things about myself.

Let's start with Levin: We've been having air raids every night lately. A couple of nights ago Levin was on airplane guard when a dive bomber broke through and dropped a buzz bomb (rocket bomb) on the runway. It did no damage and, by a freak, only one casualty—Levin caught a splinter of it in his heel, luckily just low enough to miss the joint. It did sever a tendon but the report is it can be healed.

Yesterday the planes took off for Nagoya, and Levin's crew didn't come back. They were rammed over the target during the hottest reception the 29's have met to date. (The Heavenly Body is still down with a badly cracked blister. Since the

81

blister would probably give when the ship is pressurized at altitude, we can't get up high enough to go over in formation.)

It's Levin's luck that tells me something about chance. What I think is that you can and should take all precautions, but no precaution in the world will rule out the overwhelming and forever impact of possibility and impossibility that can happen to you.

It hurts, too, to pass the bunks the boys left. Hodges, Hunt, Dreier, Nyen, Yanik. It hurts when the smiling boys go down. The smiling, and competent, and warm. The good men chance took down. You can't sympathize, by definition, until you feel a thing yourself. It hurts and it darkens to see them go. And a lot of it because it might have been anyone of us, or all of us, or me.

I don't know. I don't think I'll mind it too much. The trouble with wakening the imagination is that it makes you afraid in advance. What I discovered later is that both the imagination and the fear vanish while the thing is happening. May it never happen wrong. May what happens be always cool days when I know myself, home, the right bed, and right words for things seen and well measured.

JANUARY 5th

Tony Purtell is a good man; a draftsman, sentimental naturalist (my diagnosis), fellow GI, and good company. He works in the armament office as ordinance accountant. He misses his wife (who impresses me through his telling as a lot of real girl) and is sensible about it. He has a good head. And he has an instinct for decency without ever being the moralist. He also has a mustache, but it's irrelevant. (There's a distinction to be made. Ciardi's mustache, for instance, is impeccably relevant. Also I like his better than mine.)

I like the way he sketches. He calls himself a draftsman. Pure line. He doesn't try to use color because he's partially color blind. Instead he has developed a very satisfying draftsman's line. Taken apart his sketches seem to be a whorl of formless scrawling lines. But put together they compose. And the running sprawling line (block off a square inch of it and it looks like my fourth grade penmanship exercises) well handled, gives his pictures fluidity and movement.

I like the way he sketches, and I like him.

He did a portrait of me from memory the other night. I walked in just as he was finishing it. He looked up and immediately said: "There's what I remembered wrong." Something about two planes. The portrait was right except gaunt and more esthetic and less beef-eater than I am. He's going to do one with me sitting. I look forward to it.

We went to the movies tonight and saw *Rhapsody in Blue*, the life of Gershwin. It's the best I've seen yet from Hollywood, mostly I suspect because the music made the action and the music is good enough to do it, but there is also some well planned photography in it.

It was a strong thing to hear Gershwin again. It's too terrific. It fascinated me and suddenly it scared me. I don't want to see it again. I don't know what this sudden flood of hypersensitivity is, but somewhere it flipped a lid and scared me. I listened to the Rhapsody in Blue and thought that I didn't want to die, and came back to find a new man (MacMillan) sleeping in what had been Hodge's bed, and it scared me. I'm glad there was a Lincoln Brigade and that there are Russians. It's the right thing to hold onto.

And I'm glad, too, there are B-29's. Whenever my imagination runs cold and damp I go out and look at a B-29 for five minutes and I'm cured. It's a good thing to look at, a beautiful thing to look at, and it's pointed the right way.

We made it off the beach at last. Our first flight since Dec. 22. I was beginning to think we were ground personnel. We were originally scheduled to bomb a staging area for planes going to the Philippines from Japan—Kaniwa Jima in the Ryukyu or Nanoli Islands about 400 miles off the coast of China and about 175 Northeast of Formosa. With MacArthur on Luzon and the Philippines campaign moving to decisive stages, a well split link in the chain of Jap reinforcements would be a good fraction for our column. We were all eager to go, first, because it was a new target and all of us are new-target happy, and second, because we were promised P-51 fighter cover from the Philippines. We've never had fighter cover and were eager to see it.

And we have yet to see it. The whole show was called off and we were hauled out of bed at 0315 yesterday morning for a very rapid briefing for another mission specially ordered by Washington, a photo-recon job. Washington wants pictures and we were sent out to get them.

Seven planes were scheduled to take off at will between 0530 and 0700. Orders were to go over singly and to fly at any altitude that would get the pictures. The points scheduled for the run were Osaka, Kobe, one other city I can't recall, and Nagoya. We carried no bombs, the theory being that if the first plane dropped no bombs, defences might not be fully alerted and the following planes would have a better chance. The joker was that to get accurate pictures the ship had to be turned over to the bombsight for a regular bomb run, and a regular bomb run in these parts gets to be from 5 to 15 minutes. (In the ETO 45 seconds is a good run.) Four bomb runs in one afternoon would leave us from 20 minutes to an hour of being sitting ducks for the AA.

As per specifications our three major objectives were to get photos of an airplane engine plant in Osaki reported to produce 10% of all army airplane engines, to get photos of Kobe for future target data, and to observe the results of the recent Nagoya raids. Nagoya, one of Japan's most inflammable cities, has been showered with incendiaries and Washington wants to know the totals.

That's what we took off for, and what we didn't get. Our engines purred along just off the whitecaps. Then, when we started to climb, No. 4's supercharger went dead giving us no power from No. 4 at altitude. The turbo supercharger feeds oxygen to the engine. Without it the engine is strangled. Campbell couldn't get it started and we had to turn back when we were about 5 1/2 hours out. The procedure is always to turn back if an engine quits. Partly because you need maximum power over the target, partly because running on 3 engines boosts gas consumption 5% and our gas is figured too close to stand it.

The denouement was to land after 10 hours and have the ground crew discover that all the turbo-supercharger needed was a fuse that could have been replaced in a minute. Well, it's part of everything that happens. It's not Campbell's fault, or any one man's fault really. We're all of us poor soldiers. We're too busy being fast ball players, too full of personally staying alive and wishing we were working in a defense plant. And our whole organization is inefficient. Everything is left to the individual, and check lists are rudimentary if at all.

Case in point, I committed an error in gross negligence; put a sear slide in backwards and tested out with a dead gun when we test fired. It's an inexcusable error. One I've checked for hundreds of times and simply let slip this one time. I managed to tear open the turret in the air, strip the gun down and put the sear slide in right. Then I had the job of getting the practically inaccessible ammunition back in. With luck I got it done in a little over an hour, and so tired from standing on my toes to apply force with my fingertips that I was shaking with muscular tension. A lot less than I deserved.

We got back and I stumbled into a formless argument with Nick Brown. I was advocating ruthless area bombing (assuming we had the air power) to wipe out the factories and the workers together. My qualification was that it was regrettable but necessary, since our precision bombing seems to have everything but precision and only pattern bombing against a selected area will give us results. Nick's argument was that bombed out people would hate us so fanatically we could never handle a satisfactory peace with them. I couldn't see but what the Japanese would go on hating us fanatically anyway, and there the argument bogged down into repetition until Joe Collins began red baiting. He's a thorough gent. In fifteen minutes he managed to hit every red baiting cliche carried in standard stock by Coughlin's *Christian Front* papers, and the combined Hearst and McCormick press. (z.B "you can't change human nature," "what's the difference between communism and fascism, anyhow?" "the reds are as grabby as anyone," "why was Finland attacked," "well, they had purges, didn't they?") Among other examples of classical statement: "the human equation of greed is irreducible," "individualism is too permanent to alter," "War just proves what man is."

I gave it up.

We have 75 combat hours and are scheduled for the Air Medal, a sort of hash stripe in color.

JANUARY 15, '44

The gambling bug nipped up most of yesterday and bit me for $80 worth of next month's pay. To date I've done nothing but lose on Saipan. Ah well.

Zacchini, the mail clerk, and two or three partners have opened a gambling casino under canvas. Well, a house crap game. They made themselves a dice table, rigged some lights

86

and a tent over it, and have been going full blast since pay day making a fairly good thing of it at 25¢ per roll, that is, each shooter pays a quarter each time he gets the dice. There has been a lot of money on that table.

The officers are drunk and singing noisily. They got their weekly liquor ration yesterday. Also they put on quite a track meet. The PA system announced that 70 air mattresses were on hand in the Supply Room for issue to officers and would be given out to the first 70 comers. The huts across the way began exploding officers faster than a direct hit on a Honolulu call house with about similar results in state of dress. We stood by our doors and cheered them as they pummelled up the dust.

Last night at about 11:30 I dropped into the mess hall for coffee. I was lounging around the kitchen when Skipper and Bud walked in. Skipper had been drinking with one of the pilots who ditched and had been picked up by sub, and with the sub's commander. He was in high spirits.

With Skipper's rank to open doors and oil hinges the mess hall suddenly produced roast beef and fried eggs, peaches (canned), fruit juice, real butter, bread and coffee. We had a long loving bull session. Skipper was particularly concerned about Mike's navigation and kept wanting to know whether or not I could get us back in in case something happened to Mike. I'm sure I can with any luck at all, or even with practically none. So long as I can hit within 200 miles we can radio in. I don't possibly see how I could miss by that much.

We talked round and round in circles about one of the crews in the 497th that flatly refused to fly again (after hitting serious trouble eight times out of eight missions they couldn't take it, and all but the radioman quit—they were courtmartialled for it), and we talked about submarines (they're on the same status as flying personnel in extra pay etc. but can request change of duty at any time.) incidentally I learned that our lifeguard subs surface within 10 or 15 miles of Japan during a raid and stay

87

there for four or five hours at a stretch—knowing the Japs have picked them up on radar—and we talked about schedules—we're due to pull 35 missions. Mathematically that leaves us a fair chance at the present attrition rate. About 2 out of every 300 planes (1.5%) airborne for a mission fail to return. Accordingly the chances are 75 to 1 that we'll return from any given mission, and about 2 to 1 that we'll complete 35 missions in one piece. That's the mathematics of it as rendered. I'm not sure it's meaningful in those terms but that's how Wing sees it.

Skipper has a foul passion for raw potatoes. He munched down a couple of them as we sat shooting the GI breeze.

After Skipper went to bed, Bud and I tried to get a truck to steal some lumber with, but found an empty motor pool and had to put off our provisioning. We sat around and talked in the dark until 3:00 A.M. I like Bud. He tries to know and to understand and has the right questions. We talked about everything in enormous jumps and finally went to bed. I slept till 11:30.

JANUARY 21, '45

Nothing changes until it gets worse. Things stayed dull and static and suddenly the news is that the crew is being split up. Cordray is going up to Wing to fly a Super-Dumbo, Mike may go to group, and somebody's co-pilot is being shoved off on us as A/C. I don't like it. I won't do anything until it becomes definite, but if it goes through as first reports have it, I can't see flying. On the other hand I can't see grounding myself. Or maybe the simplest fact is that I can't see. I just don't like it.

Skipper goes up to a cushy job. A Super-Dumbo is a stripped-down 29 turned into a flying gas tank. It can stay up 24 hours and will tag behind on missions detaching itself to stand by any ship in distress, keeping it spotted for rescue. It's only armament is a tail turret, and chances are it won't need that since it doesn't go in over the target. No flak, no fighters. It makes a nice war.

We pull a last mission together tomorrow. We're standing by for a new briefing on it (it was postponed from yesterday.) According to the last briefing it's Tokyo: we go over at 25,000 (giving away 5000–7000 ft.) on a 60 mile bomb run. The target is the Mitsubishi aircraft plant. It will probably be rough, Wing smells blood and is out after more. On the last raid (Savage flew our ship) the Wing completely destroyed one aircraft factory. Now they want the same thing every time. Well, that's what we're here for—for as long as we last.

JANUARY 23

The mission was changed to Nagoya. Target: the Mitsubishi aircraft plant that we've already damaged. We were briefed to go in down the whole length of the peninsula between Kobe and Nagoya, just close enough to alert the Kobe fighters and put them on our tails even before the IP (a lake just East and North of Kobe.) From the IP to the target leaves a 60 mile bomb run through rough going. We were briefed to go in downwind giving us enough ground speed to make flak practically ineffective. But the bomb run was set for 26,000 ft.— low enough to put everything but piper cubs on our tail.

Our new pilot is Rouse—2nd Lt. former co-pilot on Hodges crew. It's a raw deal to whip him in over Orenstein's head. Major Van Tryte was scheduled to go along with us to check Rouse out as pilot. When we reached the line, however, we found No. 2 Engine non-op. I can't say I'm sorry. I don't like the idea of going in over a run as hot as Nagoya with a pilot out for a check ride.

89

The strike reports came in this afternoon. Capt. Gerwick's old crew with Major Roberts riding along had to ditch in Nagoya Harbor. The report is that they made a perfect ditching and are probably prisoners by now. The fighter opposition was—as foreknown—very heavy.

Ciardi seems to be having combat nerves. The new policy is to go in lower and lower. The object—as it should be—is to wipe out targets. But the terrific underlining of our complete expendability (we have a new CG with ideas) doesn't help much. Losses will get heavier as we commit ourselves more and more definitely to Nagoya and Tokio. No one will tell us how many missions we're expected to pull. And pilots are being hauled around and crews broken up at a terrific rate. Capt. Cordray has gone to Wing, Capt. Gerwick is grounded for physical reasons, La Marche has gone to Guam as an Instructor, Major Van Tryte has gone to Group and his crew broken up. The old 2 Capt's left are McClure and Tackett. The rest of us ride with 2nd Lt. co-pilots recently remade as airplane commanders—good men, god knows, but the boys with the rank were the boys with the stick time. So far we have lost Major Hurlbutt, Capt. Grice, Lt. Schmidt, Colonel King, Lt. Col. Mulkus, Col. Bragg, Major Roberts and whoever was riding with Roberts today.

And of course the instinct for self preservation kicks up. I find myself thinking that it's foolish to stick my neck out over Japan when my real usefulness and capability as a person and as a unit of society is in writing what needs to be written well. And I'm sure it's true and reasonable. I'd frankly bow out if I knew how to. I could go to Col. Brannock tomorrow and say I quit and be busted down to private. But I can't let myself and won't. All the same I know I'd grab at any reasonable excuse to save face. The Japanese and I. If I do get killed it will be because I lack the courage to quit and accept the humiliation of being a general duty KP. And if I come through and get back as a small fry hero it will be for the same pointless reason.

I'm frankly afraid of these lowered altitude runs. And I'm frankly afraid that Wing's refusal to tell us how many missions we're to fly means that we're here to be used up.

It's an odd and unpredictable thing. I'm calm enough in danger. I do my job and keep cool. But this waiting to be expended does me down. I have to keep thinking of the Russians. They advanced 38 miles yesterday. It's right to know they're there. I think it's the right thing to think of. If only for false courage.

It has grown to be quite a while since I made an entry. I perceive that I'm not a diary keeper by temperament. The last entry was the Nagoya mission. The early strike reports were wrong. The crew did not ditch. Their plane blew up at 8,000 ft. The Wing lost 3 others. Those that came back were shot full of holes—it's a wonder how some of them made it back at all. All praise to No. 2 Engine for stopping us.

It gave me the jitters for a while. The boys on Gerwick's old crew were boys I'd known a long while. Just a few days before I had written a letter in bad Italian for Conti's mother, a letter full of the proper filial palavers that mean the son loves his mother but has never been able to communicate with her in a living relationship. I remember thinking that it was a terrific waste to let a relationship become mother-and-son instead of person-to-person. Well, it's no longer a problem in this instance I'm afraid. It was wasted in another country.

Maybe it's because I recognized so much of my own pattern with mother in the thing. It came hard when the news

91

was made definite. A war department telegram after bullets fire and falling.

What I discover is that you have to play tricks with yourself to keep going. It produces all sorts of rationalization, and plain intellectual dishonesty. Or it can be lulled by making mechanical motions—by filling your mind up with poker, or dice or baccarat or chess or liquor or just meaningless movement. There's a lot of that sort of thing around.

The next run—which we also missed and which was also at 25,000 feet—was also to Nagoya, and fairly disastrous. All of the squadron's planes limped home, but the Wing lost 10 ships to enemy action, ditching, and crash landings. Only 29 made it in over the target. They found about 200 fighters sitting at 30,000 waiting to make passes at them.

The nearest thing to a miracle that we've had yet was Carrico's job of flying back from that one with two engines gone on the same side. No. 2 engine was shot out over the target at the same time that the nose of the ship was shot open. (The cockpit was riddled and Chico (Carrico) had a burst go between his legs, but no one was hit.) No. two's prop would not feather and ran away. Pretty soon after it hit 5000 runaway RPM's it burned off the prop shaft, pulled ahead, turned over on its side and flew over to No. one's prop, cutting it to stubs. The impact sprung the wing badly. And that's all of it except that they made it home against everything in the book that says the 29 can't fly and hold altitude on two engines. They had Franklin along as radio operator on an emergency replacement. He kept sending all the way. And with a flourish. His first message of distress caused a lot of bewilderment and seeking for mistakes in transmission, but will probably stay on in the Squadron's history: "No. 1 and No. 2 Engine gone. We're coming in. ETA 11:30 Greenwich."

"We're coming in," is the stuff newspaper legends are made of. What he confesses is that he couldn't think of any other way of saying "we're still in the air but God knows for how long and ditching would probably be suicide."

Well.

Rouse has been transferred back to his old crew as A/C. We have a new pilot—Hughes. Seems like a good man. And 27 has been taken away from us. We now share 33 (Slick Dick).

Mission tomorrow for Kobe. As a disorganized and not yet reorganized crew, we don't go. Thank you. This 25,000 ft. business is bad stuff. The B-29 has only one station that can reply to vertical attacks from above. Which means that in every series of coordinated attacks from above all but one plane can barrel down without being shot at. The Japs are making capital of the weak spot. Until we either go up to altitudes where they can't get above us, or else go in with fighter escort, losses are going to be heavy.

And, incidentally, all the low level raids have been miserable busts as bombing missions. We don't seem to have put 100 bombs on the target in three tries.

FEB. 13

I used to tell myself I was coming overseas to find out. And I used to believe without telling myself that I could pretty well guess what it would be like. The simple fact is that I couldn't have guessed at all. I don't think I even so much as realized back in the States that there was danger enough anywhere for me to die of.

Intellectually, rationally, of course. To the girl I was kissing and being profoundly moved by, I could shrug gallantly. "Of course, but you can't stay alive with fear. You can only stay alive so long as you stay unafraid." It was obviously a gesture, but I really did believe it.

I thought war was raucous and close mouthed and rigidly exact and that all men close to the fighting and dying were obscene as Marine Sgts. and hard as Hollywood desperadoes. I believed that in my fearful innocence. I never dreamed that there was gentleness and tenderness and confessed fear everywhere in it. I could never have dreamed the tenderness that breeds in war.

I am reminded of a very complex story. On New Year's Eve the Japs got a dive bomber through the Island defenses. It dropped a single rocket bomb that burst harmlessly on the coral runway. Coral is impossible to damage. What it is always possible to damage is flesh. One of the plane guards posted (nightly?) from the combat crews dove for his sandbags too late—caught a bomb fragment in the heel. It made a messy gash. It bled badly and you couldn't tell how badly because the thirsty coral-ground drank it down as fast as his body bled it. I remember thinking that these island rocks were insatiable. I had the feeling that that one coral patch could have drunk the whole blood of man without nearing its whole glut.

One of the armorers had already managed a tourniquet. By the time the ambulance arrived the bleeding was halfway under control. Leon, the wounded guard, lay pale and gentle as a ghost under the full moon, and the great bearded armorer touched his flesh with fingers light as butterflies. I shall always think of that swatch of moonlight in which we waited for the ambulance. The gunner hurt and graceful as a girl, the armorer whole and graceful and gentle as a flower.

The complication is in the sequel. We took off on a major strike against Japan on the 3rd. The armorer volunteered to replace the gunner on the crew. Over Nagoya the plane was rammed by a fighter and spilled down afire through five miles of air.

What I remember is that hurt and gentleness touched under the moon on a splatch of blood stained coral, and that gentleness died for it.

It was the unpredictable that set our mood. What but unpredictable chance transformed the armorer's concern to death over Japan. What bond with the gunner's suffering drove him to ask for the flight? He wasn't even on flying duty. And what but unpredictable chance transformed the gunners hurt into life? Wounded him to stay alive?

It is that my rationality could never have foreseen. That toying at imponderable chance. And the mute gestating touch of the armorer's pity to the gunner's hurt.

Imponderable chance became our life. Irrationally we add our losses per mission, derived percentages, forecast future losses, compute the percentages of our survival. And once we had said 50% or 30% it was as if the sybil had spoken from a cave. "Even money" we said. "Or two to one." And saying it charmed us back to belief in our physical immortality. It was inconceivable that a man could lose his immortality on an even money chance or even at two to one. We took it for assurance assured as if mathematics were a charm against chance, as if reducing it to a number made a wall against machine guns. As primitive as that.

Except that our fear was civilized. In a sense fear expands us, touches us more closely together. Fear gentled us even while mentality disappeared from our lives.

And

FEB. 16, '45

Journal of the possible turning:

Yesterday began like a day with intentions. Terrific convoys have been moving in and out, Tanapey harbor is clotted with ships, naval ships, and carriers. We had been briefed for Nagoya in a two-wing formation of 120 planes (The 313th wing is now operating from Tinian).

95

(The 313th incidentally is a rush job. And has paid for it. Their training was cut to nothing to rush them over here. As a result they bled. On their first raid they sent 34 ships, lost one to enemy action and eight operationally—one crashed on take off, two collided over the target while flying formation, three ditched, and two are missing, probably ditched. The one that crashed on take off killed all the crew and one ground man, 100 men and nine ships lost on the first run. Comment? No comment.)

Anyhow there was something in the wind. We were briefed to expect the Navy anywhere along the route and we were emphatically warned not to mention it even on interphone. The target was a Mitsubishi engine plant and with 120 planes we were expected to clean it off the map.

It was quite a sight. I'd never seen so many 29's at once, and when we hit the wing assembly point where Tinian joined us, the sky was full of them. It's something of a problem to assemble that many planes in a formation and keep out of one another's prop wash. It worked out very well, and we left the assembly point in good order.

The pilots have been overusing the VHF inter-plane communication set and everybody was warned not to use it except in emergencies. A major rode in one of the planes to make complete recordings of all VHF communications. The boys knew it and the talky ones behaved. The air was beautifully clear.

(Incidental: our assembly point was a rock about 10 feet high, very jagged, and about 100 feet wide by 300 ft. long. On it we sighted a Jap Betty. Mystery. It couldn't have landed— the landing gear was intact and nothing but a crash landing was possible. We had a good look and I suspect it was a dummy. But why plant a dummy on a rock in mid-Pacific. Very mysterious, very mysterious.)

We left the assembly point in good order and almost immediately hit into a heavy front. From there on for 500 miles into

Japan visibility was zero and the formation completely disintegrated. VHF discipline disintegrated simultaneously and the air was full of calls. The major and his recording set transcribed some beautiful absurdities and downright stupidities.

We weren't too free of stupidities ourself. Capt. La Marche rode with us so Hughes co-piloted. We came out of the soup and hit the coast alone and looked around for someone to hitch onto. Far off to the right we saw 2 29's, and closer to the left 3 more. I thought La Marche would at least hook onto one of those elements. It didn't help any when he decided to go in alone. Alone over Nagoya and S-2 had briefed us to expect 200 fighters (Subtitle Goddamming the Pilot down the Hottest Spot in Asia.) In we went.

Anticlimatically nothing happened. Tokio radio today announced that the B-29's had uncorked a new very confusing series of formations. Very confusing. We started on our bomb run and by the time we had dropped our bombs we intersected bomb runs by five other elements of 29's going in at every level and on every heading. To keep things interesting, a last element of four planes dropped their bombs right across our nose.

Meanwhile no fighters pulling out over Nagoya. We had two half-hearted attacks that veered off as soon as we fired a warning burst. The Japs must have been as confused as we were. But it was still a fool stunt of La Marche's to go in alone when everything he knew in advance indicated about 200 fighters waiting. So we live. (With luck. Without luck it's so we die.)

The VHF comedy of errors really piled up as we headed back. Sample transcripts from 500 miles of solid soup.

I.

"Mascot 4-8 to Mascot 3-7."

"Mascot 3-7. Come in. Where are you Bill?"

"Who the hell knows?"

"What's your altitude?"

"Hey, don't send that in the clear."

"O.K. What's your angels? How many angels have you?"

"I'm at 28,000 feet."

II.

Mickey Mouse Leader, Mickey Mouse 3-zero to Mickey
Mouse Leader.

This is M.M.L. come in MM 3-zero."

"M.M.L. I am in the clear over the coast at 28,000 feet. I
have a four plane element. Have you any target instructions?"

Long pause. Then . . .

"M.M. 3-zero take your element and _____." Pause.

He must have changed his mind. What he said finally was
"Take your element and bomb a coastal town in Japan."

"Roger. I have it. Do you understand. I have a four plane
element and am over the coast at 28,000 ft."

"Friend," said M.M.L., "the whole damn Jap Empire
understands it."

The Japs must have enjoyed it. They even tried to join the
party. At one point a heavily Oriental voice pidgeoned in
to Mickey Mouse Leader inventing a code Identification of
his own:

"Mickey Mouse Leader, this is Sally Rand. What are your
intentions?"

M.M.L. didn't answer. Ah, if only he'd been man enough
to reply: "The low element of the 17th wave will go in at
65,000 feet and release their parachute rockets at 3 second
intervals. Bonzai!"

Well, the Major and his recording machine heard everything else on that run.

And since then history milestones. All the Navy hush-hush
has broken. The Fleet had moved in under the front we rode,
and today 1200 carrier based planes were dogfighting over

Japan and laying here an egg there an egg. My guess is that it's no hit and run raid. Prophecy: the fleet and the carriers will stay where it (they) is (are) until the Japanese Navy comes out to object. At which time the objection will be overruled and the fleet can go on staying there. It's wonderful to think what must be happening to a lot of fighters that won't be shooting us down hereafter. Bells for the Navy. I may get back home yet.

There were disquieting rumors about the new general. Washington had drafted him from the China-Burma-India B-29's to whip us into shape. Our first raid had even drawn a speech from Gen. Arnold. "The issue has been joined. Japan shall be struck again and again. (Fanfares) She has sown the wind and she shall reap the wild wind."

But the truth was that we hadn't done too well. The new General was a shake up and he came on a dark rumor with the reputation of having achieved the best bombing results and the heaviest losses of any commander in the Air Forces.

His first order was to lower our bombing altitude from 30,000 to 25,000.

I am not a soldier. If I conceive myself to be anything I am a civilian accepting the risks and restrictions necessary to doing a job that must be done before I can return to my own patterns. I don't know what a soldier would think. I have only met one professional soldier—a Capt. from West Point, a pilot who was the perfect military in all things except piloting his plane. May the abracadabra of chance watch over his crew. I distrust professional soldiers.

My civilian reaction to the general's order was what everyone I knew felt. "This man I have never seen will very likely be what kills me," I thought. I felt it was a far darker certainty when the next semi-official rumor followed. "The targets will be hit and wiped out. If the bombardiers cannot hit them from 25,000, the missions will be run at 20,000, and if they cannot hit them at 20,000 they will go in at 15,000 but the targets will be hit."

That was the night I sat down and wrote a letter home to be mailed in case I didn't come back.

IIA.

30,000 or 25,000. What loomed so dark in the issue of 5,000 feet? The general was one school of thought. The men who had the mission to fly made another.

Remember that our missions were flown against two enemies. The Japanese AA batteries and fighters made one enemy. The other was 3,000 round trip miles of Pacific Ocean. There was the third enemy too—metal was our enemy. Its tiniest flaw, its first imperfection waited to drop us from air. A loose bolt or a split rivet might spring the sequence that would end in our symmetry's ruin. In every engine there is fire and death in more places than any eye can find, and it waits forever.

The issue made in favor of lowering our altitude was that too many planes had been forced to ditch due to mechanical failure. The statisticians pointed out that the added 5000 feet strained the already strained engines to the point of no margin of safety. The verdict was that we would lose more planes over the target, but fewer to the Pacific Ocean. The ground and staff officers were unanimously agreed.

The flying teams saw it differently. Our bombers were built for altitude. At 36,000 feet attacking fighters were reduced in efficiency to the point where we could laugh them off, and the flak was that much less accurate. Even if the added strain brought on mechanical failure, the crew still had a chance to

100

make a ditching and be rescued by the life guard subs and destroyers. And time and again we cited fighters that had risen to meet us and couldn't quite make the last few thousand feet. The extra 5000 feet was our margin for life. In it we saw home again, and warmth, and wife-flesh, and neon, and country furrows, and the lost language.

Actually neither argument mattered. We were on the Island to destroy Japanese factories and Japanese factories had a price tag attached. We were the price and neither longing nor the will to live mattered in the final balance. The General was our bargainer; he bid for those factories at the asking price, and he signed to pay for them in the universal currency that in the end is the currency that buys all of the world—human life. However we revere the idea of it in the Western World, nothing in practice is cheaper. With it we buy tunnels under the Hudson, steel rails across the Mississippi, skyscrapers in New York, bridge heads in France, factories in Japan. I am reminded of Melville's observation in *Moby Dick*, that not a gallon of sperm oil came ashore to light the lamps of America but a drop of human blood went with it. War only emphasizes it by numbers. To buy one coral rock suitable for air-strips and strategically located: 3,972 lives, 5,764 wounds. To destroy one Japanese oil refinery, damage one toolshed, kill an incidental number of civilians, drop three bombs on an assembly plant, crater so many nearby fields—price blank bombers, blank times eleven men. Those losses we can read and weep and fear. They lift in headlines and stun us sober. But what of the other purchase? To buy one bus line from San Francisco to Fresno—one driver twelve passengers. To supplying one plant with latex for rubber—six natives, 23 seamen. To providing nitro for one oil well—one driver. The final price for all things whether it be Japanese factories or Brazilian coffee for your breakfast is human life. We revere it and sanctify its importance, yet there is nothing we spend so lavishly. Was a ship wrecked to bring you your coffee? You will go on drinking your two cups per morning. There is no taste of the corpse in it, as there is no taste of death in the pure air of the sun. It is death to breathe it because without it there is no life, no motion.

The General is part of the motion, as completely of the motion as we are. But none of us can believe his smallness. Each of us is his own world's center of seeing and waiting and longing. We cannot stop the fear. Twenty of us sit in a room for an hour and once in the hour each of us will think and put away the thought that ten of us will be dead before the other ten come alive. We are moats in a current. And we are suns to our cosmic systems. And we wait with dread fringing all our consciousness.

We are buying the world's goods in the open market and each man is appalled at finding himself part of the price.

———————

MARCH 5, '45

We now have 9 missions. Eight over Japan, one over Iwo. I've slipped up for a long while on the journal—tropical inertia. Since flying with La Marche, we have two day strikes over Tokio and a night run over Tokio.

The night strike was a searchlight run. Nothing else came up at us. Who's mad? Fighters and flak may break my back, but searchlights'll never hurt me.

Rouse was shot down over Tokio on the day strike. A good boy—it hurts. Outside of that bad luck these missions have been easy. The Navy is also striking away at Japan. The Marines are taking Iwo—bloodily. When Iwo is taken we'll have fighter escort.

I made Staff as of 3/1/45. We're in for the Air Medal. And—climactically—the rumor is that Lt. Col. Brannock has the whole squadron in for the Good Conduct Ribbon. That I have to see.

The boys are just back from a razzle-dazzle play over Tokio. They left a general conflagration behind them.

Orders for it came through yesterday: 300 planes of the 73rd, 313th, and 314th were briefed in at 5000-7000 ft. Each plane carried 40 350 lb. incendiary clusters. Bomb-bay tanks were removed—since the planes were not going to altitude they could do it on their wing tanks. To save weight all guns and ammunition were stripped out. Only two gunners went along.

Hughes asked for two volunteers. Tiger immediately volunteered. I volunteered to cut high card with T. J. and Chico. I guess I'm not the volunteer type. Back at the Quonsett, Chico refused to cut. We had a flare up, and I said the hell with it I'd go, but I wanted no future part of any crew Chico was on. The next think I knew Chico had his stuff aboard in a spite: he was flying it by God, but he was off the crew as soon as the ship landed. I can't keep track of all these moves and countermoves.

The planes hit at 3:00 A.M. All ours got through. Reports are inconclusive, but it must have been terrific. The crew was in the second of 9 waves and smoke was already 2000 ft above their altitude (7000). While Tokio burns—there's another one called for tomorrow night.

All rumor and disquiet waited for the General's first briefing. It came two days after his arrival.

The crews gathered in the tin-roofed group briefing building and what had been disquiet became certainty. Target:

103

Nagoya. Altitude: 25,000 ft. A serious young Major discussed the type of formation, a spectacled 2nd Lt. rambled on about weather and decided it was too uncertain to forecast definitely until just before take off time, the communications officer stated frequencies, the radar officer gave instructions, the intelligence officer stuttered nothing, the armament officer recited the bomb loads. Almost you might believe they saw their pointlessness. Then you perceived that the mechanical men would never fully grasp their pointlessness.

It didn't matter. No one was listening. All thoughts stayed with the lines the group navigator had drawn and explained on the map of Japan.

Through all the chaotic series of attendant officers of radio, radar, bomb and camera, the map sat on everyone's mind, waiting.

THE
POEMS

Dec. 16, '44

Elegy for a Cove Full of Bones
– Saipan

Tibia, tarsal, skull, and shin:
Bones come out where the guns go in.
Hermit crabs like fleas in armor
Crawl the coral-pock, a tremor
Moves the sea, and surf falls cold
On coves where glutton rats grow bold.
In the brine of sea and weather
Shredded flesh transforms to leather,
And the wind and sea invade
The rock-smudge that the flame throwers made.

Death is lastly a debris
Folding on the folding sea:
Blankets, boxes, belts, and bones,
And a jelly on the stones.
What the body taught the mind
~~Flies~~ Ants explore and do not find.
Here the certain stood to die,
Passionately to prove a lie.

The poems included here were written on Saipan in the pages of this diary. After the war, "Poem for my Twenty-ninth Birthday," "Ritual for Singing Bat," and "Elegy Just in Case" appeared in *Other Skies* by John Ciardi (Little Brown, 1947). "Elegy for a Cove Full of Bones" was first published in *Poetry* in 1988.

Poem for my Twenty-ninth Birthday

Once more the predawn throbs on engine sound
Down coral slope, papaya grove, and pine,
Into the sea whose pastures girdle round
The native in his jungle, I in mine,
And you in yours, O gentle stay-at-home:
Your talons, too, have raked the living bone.

We waken, and the cities of our day
Move down a cross-haired bomb sight in the mind.
The thoughtless led, those only in the way,
The powerful by intent, wake there and find
Their jungles closing, each man tangled tight
Into this day that may not last till night.

Now I have named another year of time
Learning to count not mine but a world's age.
And on the morning of no birth I climb
To sign in fire your and my heritage:
The bomb whose metal carcass dressed and bled
Is our day's gift to populate the dead.

See from his living garden, damp with dawn,
The native turn from weeding as we pass
His centuries upon this flowering stone.
Our trucks arrived in clouds of dust and gas
Coat his green jungle till the daily rain.
He sees us past and turns to weed again.

His is the simplest darkness, our grotesque
Of straps and buckles, parachutes and guns,
Our gear of kit and cartridge, helmet, mask,
Life vest, rations, and the elegance
Of all our conscious gestures and our gum,
Darken us further than his guess can come.

We leave his green past. On a metal din
Our gears resolve us from the valley night.
To plateaus where the rapt emblazoned fin
Our perfect bomber lifts to the first light
Mounts on the air up which the morning sun
Prophesies Asia and a death to come.

Already now, my dear, this turning sun
Has been your day, and here returns to me
Where I inherit on a bomber's run
Your image from the sundial of the sea.
I dream you smiling, waking fleshed in grace,
And see, a gun sight photographs your face.

I cannot lose my darkness. Posed and dressed,
I touch the metal womb our day will ride.
We take our places while a switch is pressed,
And sun and engines rise from the hillside—
A single motion and a single fire
To burn, return, and live upon desire.

Look at the sea and learn how malice shines
Bright as a noon come down through colored glass.
We are the soaring madness of our times
Marking our own flown never-ending loss.
The whitecaps strewn like lint on a stone floor
Wait, will swallow, close, and wait once more.

Now, westering, our day has named its course:
Far down in frost and tiny symmetry
Fuji, the magic mountain of what was,
Places our past on the trajectory
Of the co-sined and wind-computed fall
Our bombs descend to save or kill us all.

What has been lost when once the bomb is flown?
(We fire at fighters and await the rose
Blossoming in fire upon the town
Whose living history we have come to close.)
The dead are not our loss. My memory is
Our simplest day was guiltier than this.

Our innocence shall haunt our murderous end
Longer than statues or the tabled walls
Alphabetized to death. Shall we pretend
Destruction moves us or that death appalls?
Are we the proud avengers time returned?
—We dreamed by all the windows while time burned.

Now, our intention bloodied late by need,
We sit our jungles hemispheres apart;
I, blossomed awkwardly from dragon seed,
You, endlessly the pure and gentle heart.
And death run loose like shadows in a wind
On all the reasoned motions of the mind.

And, last, by dark, we have our rock again:
Our wheels touch and our waiting lives return.
Far off the dead are lying in the rain,
And on their dark the ruined cities burn
Our jungles down with light enough to see
The last compassionate necessity.

Ritual for Singing Bat

"One part Indian, one part Tennessee,"
He said his first day in. We saw him dive,
His feather dress of flame ceremoniously
Prompt to the ritual of the pyre-borne dove.
"You can't quite kill a man named Singing Bat,"
He said. And would have bet. And lost the bet.

Simply as tomahawks had spelled his tribe,
Or guns snicked out the great-grandmother's clan,
Chance would not take a totem's bribe
To pass the dice on one Tennessee man.
Stones will not break completely, but they break.
And a Tennessee man with a gun, make no mistake,

Will crumble less than any battered stone.
He passed into an orange feather dress
From a white sky to a yellow emperor's town.
Bombs opened back like blossoms in the place
Below the black plumed arrow that he rode
Into the misty forest of a cloud.

He never reappeared. Whether our sight
Fixed to an angle's logic, logically
Lost him, or whether totems plumed and bright
Demanded one last mystery from the sky—
A fluff of cloud closed on him and returned
A legend only for the flesh that burned.

Bat, may your bones be diamonded like dice,
And all your blood be whisky fragrantly
Sloshed in a jug of clay, while on the skies
You rattle naturals through eternity,
And every roll be thunder, bet and faded,
For a Tennessee man who shot the sky—and made it.

Elegy Just in Case

Here lie Ciardi's pearly bones
In their ripe organic mess.
Jungle blown, his chromosomes
Breed to a new address.

Was it bullets or a wind
Or a rip-cord fouled on Chance?
Artifacts the natives find
Decorate them when they dance.

Here lies the sgt.'s mortal wreck
Lily spiked and termite kissed,
Spiders pendant from his neck
And a beetle on his wrist.

Bring the tic and southern flies
Where the land crabs run unmourning
Through a night of jungle skies
To a climeless morning.

And bring the chalked eraser here
Fresh from rubbing out his name.
Burn the crew-board for a bier.
(Also Colonel what's-his-name.)

Let no dice be stored and still.
Let no poker deck be torn.
But pour the smuggled rye until
The barracks threshold is outworn.

File the papers, pack the clothes,
Send the coded word through air—
"We regret and no one knows
Where the sgt. goes from here."

"Missing as of inst. oblige,
Deepest sorrow and remain—"
Shall I grin at persiflage?
Could I have my skin again

Would I choose a business form
Stilted mute as a giraffe,
Or a pinstripe unicorn
On a cashier's epitaph?

Darling, darling, just in case
Rivets fail or engines burn,
I forget the time and place
But your flesh was sweet to learn.

Swift and single as a shark
I have seen you churn my sleep;
Now if beetles hunt my dark
What will beetles find to keep?

Fractured meat and open bone—
Nothing single or surprised.
Fragments of a written stone,
Undeciphered but surmised.

One Betty—Five Skulls

The search lights caught your enemy and mine.
Balboa's ocean lit with tracer's dawn.
Guns yammered and the falling surf returned
A moment's sound through gunfire and was gone.

Clocks counted, and from sand-bagged coral holes
We were the clocks, and all the sky was lit.
A single eastern star not in the east
Hovered and plunged, and our cheers followed it.

It fell to its own furnace, broke, and blew.
A mountain lit, and flame reached back to fly.
A moment only. Then the surf renewed
And searchlights cracked and splintered from the sky.

Fast as our cheers we trampled down the night
Racing to find the blackened plow of soil,
Where scattered in the tinfoil ruin of parts
Metal and flesh smoked in a strew of oil.

Perfectly by Orion and The Cross
The mountain darkened and the flesh burned down.
The night healed, sirens beckoned us alive
And on the hills the warning lights came on.

No angers met, no flesh touched flesh and cursed,
Drew blood, reeled back, and had its hatred learned.
But in a solitude of stars, our enemy
Turned down a wheel of dials, and fell, and burned.

Visibility Zero

All day with mist against the hurdling wind
The lights hung dressed in halves and a blur.
Air that was solid on a hurtling wing
Hangs sodden, and the parked planes wear like fur
Their look of waiting in the liquid pause
Of cloud descended, in a veil of gauze
The three complete and only trees incite
Their separate loss into the early night

Fixed to the gauge that swears we cannot see,
Our engines, blind as junk, await the light.
Cards, dice, and spinning coins turn noisily
Into the separate corners of the night.
This was the day we saw our lives made safe,
The day no engines burned and no one gave
A morning thought to chance, but late in bed
Praised the tiered fog that nowhere touched the dead.

Complete in pause, we woke into no need,
Turned back to sleep, stayed dry, and wished for mail.
Ate, and addressed a holiday—a nod
To cancelled schedules, and a word to tell
Our postponed fear that it was not our choice.
And then, released, the barracks lounging voice
In praise of hours where instruments agree
We need not waken and we need not see.

Return

Once more the searchlights beckon from the night
The homing drone of bombers. One by one
They strike like neon down the plastic dome
Of darkness palaced on our sea and sight
Where avenues of light flower on a stone
To bring the theorem and its thunder home.

Wheels touch and snub, and on the wing's decline
From air and motion into mass and weight
Grace falls from metal like a dancer's glove
Dropped from the hand. She pauses for the sign
Of one more colored light, and home and late
Crosses to darkness like an end of love.

Under the celebration of the sky
Still calling home the living to their pause
The hatches spill the lucky and returned
Onto the solid stone of not-to-die
And see their eyes are lenses and they house
Reel after reel of how a city burned.

Elegy for a Cove Full of Bones
 —Saipan
 Dec. 16, '44

Tibia, tarsal, skull, and shin:
Bones come out where the guns go in.
Hermit crabs like fleas in armor
Crawl the coral-pock, a tremor
Moves the sea, and surf falls cold
On coves where glutton rats grow bold.
In the brine of sea and weather
Shredded flesh transfers to leather,
And the wind and sea invade
The rock-smudge that the flame throwers made.

Death is lastly a debris
Folding on the folding sea:
Blankets, boxes, belts, and bones,
And a jelly on the stones.
What the body taught the mind
Flies explore and do not find.
Here the certain stood to die
Passionately to prove a lie.
At the end a covenant's pall
Of stones made solid, palpable,
Moves the victory to the sea,
And the wind indifferently.

Hate is nothing, pity less.
Angers lead us to digress:
I shall murder if I can.
Spill the jellies of a man.
Or be luckless and be spilled
In the wreck of those killed.

Nothing modifies our end:
Nothing in the ruin will mend.
If I moralize, forgive:
Error is the day we live.
In the ammoniac coves of death
I am choked for living breath.
I am tired of thinking guns,
Knowing where the bullet runs.
I am dreaming of a kiss
And a flesh more whole than this.
I am pondering a root
To destroy the cove-rat's loot.
I am measuring a place
For the living's living grace.
I am running from the breath
Of the vaporing coves of death.
I have seen our failure in
Tibia, tarsal, skull, and shin.

APPENDICES

People and Nicknames

CAPT. BERWICK   CAPT. JAMES A. GERWICK
Aircraft Commander, 500th Bomb Group.

BLAKELY*   SGT. ALTON E. BLAKELY
Radio Operator on same flight crew and barracks mate with Ciardi.

LT. COL. BRANNOCK   LT. COL. JOSEPH F. BRANNOCK
Commanding Officer, 882nd Bomb Squadron. (This is the unit to which Ciardi and his crew were assigned.)

NICK BROWN   NOT IDENTIFIABLE

COL. BRAGG   NOT IDENTIFIABLE

COL. BRUGGE   NOT IDENTIFIABLE
Probably assigned to 73 Bombardment Wing, Operations Staff-Passenger in Z □ 1 when Col. King with Major Goldsworthy and crew was shot down. (Col. King and most others survived and spent rest of war in POW camps.)

CAMPBELL   CAPT. ROBERT W. (BOB) CAMPBELL
Flight Engineer on same flight crew as Ciardi; retired as Lt. Colonel.

BARRY CAMPBELL   SGT. BARRY S. CAMPBELL

CAPTAIN/SKIPPER   CAPT. ROBERT M. (MAC) CORDRAY
Aircraft Commander of flight crew to which Ciardi was assigned; retired as Colonel.

LT. CARRICO   LT. FRANK CARRICO
Aircraft Commander, 882nd Bomb Squadron.

COL. CAUSLAND   NOT IDENTIFIABLE
Probably Commander at Kearney (NEB) Army Air Forces Base.

CG   BRIG. GEN. EMMETT (ROSEY) O'DONNELL
Commander, 73 Bombardment Wing (VH); retired as General.

JOE COLLINS   NOT IDENTIFIABLE

CONTI   CPL. JOSEPH P. CONTE

LT. COL. DOUGHERTY   LT. COL. JACK DOUGHERTY
Promoted to Colonel while in command of 500th Bombardment
Group; retired as Brigadier General.

DP   GIRLFRIEND

DREIER   NOT IDENTIFIABLE
Probably barracks mate with Ciardi.

FRANKLIN*   SGT. LLOYD W. (FRANK) FRANKLIN
Radio operator on same flight crew and barracks mate with Ciardi.

GRICE   CAPT. CHARLES G. GRISE

GROW*   LT. LYNN W. (DOC) GROW
Bombardier on same flight crew as Ciardi.

HODGE   NOT IDENTIFIABLE
Probably barracks mate with Ciardi.

HUGHES*   2ND LT. LEONARD I. HUGHES
Replaced Capt. Cordray as Aircraft Commander.

HUNT   NOT IDENTIFIABLE
Probably barracks mate with Ciardi.

HURLBUTT   MAJ. HURLBUTT
                     (COMPLETE NAME UNAVAILABLE)
One of three Flight Commanders along with Maj. Van Trigt and
Capt. Cordray of the 882nd Bomb Squadron.

ROBINSON JEFFERS
American poet.

JOHNSON*   CPL. RICHARD G. (TIGER) JOHNSON
Gunner on same flight crew and barracks mate with Ciardi.

KAUFMAN   SGT. RUSSELL L. KAUFMAN

COL. KING   COL. RICHARD T. (DICK) KING, JR.
Commanding Officer, 500th Bombardment Group (VH).

LAMARSHE   MAJ. AUSTIN W. LAMARCHE
Aircraft Commander, 500th Bombardment Group.

LEVINE   NOT IDENTIFIABLE
Probably barracks mate with Ciardi.

MCCLURE   NOT IDENTIFIABLE
Obviously not Maj. Glenn McClure, 500th Bombardment Group Adjutant.

MOORE/T. J.*   SGT. T. J. MOORE
Top Gunner on same flight crew and barracks mate with Ciardi.

TED MORRISON   THEODORE MORRISON
American novelist, poet, and for twenty-five years Director of the Bread Loaf Writers' Conference.

LT. COL. MULKUS   NOT IDENTIFIABLE

NYON   NOT IDENTIFIABLE
Probably barracks mate with Ciardi.

O'HARA*   LT. EDWIN R. (MIKE) O'HARA
Navigator on same flight crew with Ciardi.

ORENSTEIN   LT. MILTON G. (BUD) ORENSTEIN
Pilot on same flight crew with Ciardi.

PURTELL   TONY PURTELL
Ordinance accountant in armament office.

ROBERTS   MAJ. ROBERTS
With Capt. Gerwick's old crew.

ROUSE   NOT IDENTIFIABLE

SALOZ/CHICO*   SGT. CLYDE P. SALEZ
Tail gunner on same flight crew and barracks mate with Ciardi.

CAPT. SAVAGE   CAPT. JOSEPH M. (JOE) SAVAGE, JR.
Aircraft Commander, 882nd Bomb Squadron.

LT. SCHMIDT   LT. ROBERT C. SCHMIDT

SMITH   M/SGT. SIDNEY F. (SMITTY) SMITH
Ground crew chief.

WALLY STEGNER   WALLACE STEGNER
American novelist.

TACKETT   CAPT. CECIL E. TACKETT

VAN TRYTE   MAJ. JOHN R. VAN TRIGT
One of three Flight Commanders (along with Maj. Hurlbutt and Capt. Cordray) of 882nd Bomb Squadron.

WARFEL   FRANZ WERFEL
Nineteenth century Austrian novelist and poet.

ALEXANDER WOLCOTT   ALEXANDER WOOLLCOTT
American journalist and writer.

MAJ. WOLLCOTT   MAJ. WOLCOTT
Adjutant, 882nd Bomb Squadron.

YANIK   NOT IDENTIFIABLE
Probably barracks mate with Ciardi.

ZACCHINI   NOT IDENTIFIABLE
Mail clerk.

Killed in action

128

Acronyms and Initials

AA   ANTI-AIRCRAFT FIRE

A/C   AIRPLANE COMMANDER

ATC   AIR TRANSPORT COMMAND

CFC   CENTRAL FIRE CONTROL SYSTEM
Advanced electronic aiming system for controlling and firing the five turrets on a B-29. (Interconnected turrets contained twelve 50-caliber machine guns and one 20-millimeter rapid-firing cannon.)

CG   COMMANDING GENERAL

DNIF   DOWN NOT IN FUNCTION

HE   HIGH EXPLOSIVE

KP   KITCHEN POLICE

S-2   SQUADRON INTELLIGENCE OFFICE

SNAFU   SITUATION NORMAL ALL FOULED UP

T.O.   TABLE OF ORGANIZATION

VHF   VERY HIGH FREQUENCY RADIO
Used for short-range (line of sight) plane-to-plane and ship-to-ship voice communication.

X   EXTRA CREW MEMBER
Probably along on a flight for mission credit.

z.B.   German equivalent of "for example."

Places

APOE   Aerial Port of Embarkation.

Bonins Is.   Island group south and east of Tokyo.

ETO   European Theater of Operations.

Kearney   Kearney Army Air Base, Kearney, Nebraska, staging base for preparation for overseas movement.

Lowery   Lowery Army Air Base, Denver, Colorado, gunnery and electronics training base.

Off Limits   Officially prohibited to military personnel.

P of E   Port of Embarkation.

Pagan Is.   Island in northern Marianas north of Saipan.

Truk   Japanese occupied island about 600 miles southeast of Saipan.

Volcano Is.   Island group south of Bonins (includes Iwo Jima).

Things, etc.

Betty   Japanese twin-engine bomber.

Charlie   Generic term for marauding enemy planes (not full-scale attack).

Form 1A   Maintenance Status of Aircraft Report.

Mene, mene, tekel, upharsin   The handwriting on the wall from The Book of Daniel, 5:25.

QM Depot   Quartermaster Depot (a supply depot).

Sally, Nick, Irving   Type of Japanese aircraft.

Shavetail   A second lieutenant.

Suntans   A summer blouse, part of the uniform.

Towing Caterpillar   A rubber tracked vehicle for towing large aircraft on the ground.

Wing   73rd Bombardment Wing (VH).

Zeke   Japanese single-engine fighter.

Z☐1, Z☐26, etc.   Designations of planes. A, T, V, and Z indicated bomb groups; ☐ indicated the 73rd bomb wing; numbers were the tail numbers of individual planes.